THE RETURN OF INFLATION

The Return of

INFLATION

*Money and Capital in the
21st Century*

PAUL MATTICK

REAKTION BOOKS

For Ethel Shipton and Nate Cassie,
whose gift of friendship
materially aided this book's composition

Published by
REAKTION BOOKS LTD
Unit 32, Waterside
44–48 Wharf Road
London N1 7UX, UK
www.reaktionbooks.co.uk

First published 2023
Copyright © Paul Mattick 2023

Printed and bound in Great Britain by TJ Books Ltd, Padstow, Cornwall

A catalogue record for this book is available from the British Library

ISBN 978 1 78914 791 9

Contents

Monetary phenomena leave no one indifferent. They fascinate and worry everyone. On the one hand, money is surrounded by such a cloud of mystery that handling it and studying it seem to the non-expert to be esoteric activities that an ordinary person can't understand. On the other hand, money is the social reality that penetrates everyone's private life in the most intimate way, tearing apart the most solid friendships, demolishing the best-established moral positions. Faced with the enigma of money, economists and politicians are no better off than the man in the street.

—MICHEL AGLIETTA and ANDRÉ ORLÉAN,
La violence de la monnaie

Introduction

"IF THE ECONOMY LOOKS UNCLEAR TO YOU," an article by an economics reporter for the *Washington Post* began in early November 2022, "rest assured—it looks that way to the people in charge of stabilizing it too." Specifically,

> When the Federal Reserve raised interest rates yet again this week, the central bank's case for how it would tackle inflation without causing a recession boiled down to: It's unclear. What are the odds of avoiding a recession? "Hard to say," conceded Chair Jerome H. Powell. How high will interest rates go? "Very uncertain." In an hour-long news conference on Wednesday, Powell said "don't know" four times.[1]

Though the frank acknowledgement of ignorance is a recent note, economists have a long record of theoretical and predictive failure.[2] On November 5, 2008—to take a famous instance—while inaugurating a new building at the London School of Economics in the midst of the most spectacular economic collapse since 1929, Queen Elizabeth II of the UK took the opportunity to ask the assembled distinguished economists,

"Why did nobody see [the financial crisis] coming?"[3] In a published reply, a group of economists confessed that "the failure to foresee the timing, extent and severity of the crisis and to head it off, while it had many causes, was principally a failure of the collective imagination of many bright people, both in this country and internationally, to understand the risks to the system as a whole."[4] The confession of lack of imagination seems inadequate as an explanation of the predictive failure of something supposed to be a science. But it is true that blindness about the coming collapse was shared by the profession as a whole, though what was missed was not just the timing and severity but the fact of systemic instability itself. The contrast with climate science, which must analyze phenomena of comparable (if not greater) complexity but which has predicted quite accurately the shape of the coming catastrophes (though possibly not the speed with which they are arriving), is striking.

This spectacular failure was followed by further blows to the self-esteem of economics as a field. But by now economists seem to be getting used to it. Many had expected that the massive increase in budget deficits and national debts incurred to deal with the 2008 crisis would unleash damaging levels of inflation, surging interest rates, and loss of confidence in the dollar. When these evils did not make an appearance, economists—without having much to say about why—took a newly blithe tone on the relation between deficits and inflation. To give a distinguished example, Olivier Blanchard, formerly of the International Monetary Fund and now a Senior Fellow at the free-trade-boosting Peterson Institute for International Economics, asserted breezily, "At this stage, I think, nobody is very worried about debt. It's clear that we can probably go where we are going, which is debt ratios above

100 percent [of GDP] in many countries. And that's not the end of the world."⁵ According to Kenneth Rogoff, a Harvard expert on government debt and economic growth whose work was frequently cited in support of deficit reduction under President Obama, "Any sensible policy is going to have us racking up the deficit for a long time, if you can. If we go up another $10 trillion, I wouldn't even blink at that now."⁶ The cognitive dissonance was perhaps most clearly embodied in remarks by Maya MacGuineas, the president of the Committee for a Responsible Federal Budget, who urged her fellow American experts both that "We should think and worry about the deficit an awful lot, and we should proceed to make it larger."⁷

But this relaxed attitude was not to last. After a decade of wondering why inflation was so low, 2021 found economists wondering why it was suddenly so high. In the words of an economics writer for the *Los Angeles Times*, by the spring of that year "Economists [were] getting a dose of humility on forecasting inflation" as prices rose "well beyond the expectations of Wall Street and policymakers."⁸ There was widespread disagreement about the reasons for this. Was it, as one faction of economists insisted, the delayed result of the government's massive infusion of cash into the economic system since the Great Recession? Or was the inflation "temporary," in the catchphrase of the moment, due to the disruption of economic affairs by the COVID-19 pandemic in 2020–21, which had, for instance, produced shifts in demand from services to goods and an overstressing of global supply chains? Federal Reserve chairman Jerome Powell originally insisted on the temporary nature of the problem, but shifted after a few months to the idea that it must be treated as a more structural one. As a result, the upsurge of inflation, however unsettled the question of its cause, was met by trotting out time-worn diagnostic and policy recipes. The lack of any generally agreed systematic explanation for either the low inflation of the recent past or the surging numbers of the subsequent period has not prevented economists and officials from blaming rising prices on excess demand, for which the solution is supposed to be partly closing the valve on the money supply and raising interest rates.

When professional economists—as many do—openly confess their ignorance about the current dynamics of inflation, a non-professional may as well weigh in on the subject. An outsider may even have the advantage of an imagination unconstrained by professional dogma. In fact, in attempting to understand ongoing economic developments, I have been struck by the extreme disconnection between economic theory and what seem to a non-professional eye evident facts about the nature of modern society. The significance of the idea of "excessive demand," for instance in a society like that of the United States, with a quarter of the population officially living in poverty, is at the least bewildering; while the widely suggested notion that wages, rising from decades of decline and stagnation at a rate well below that of consumer prices, may be driving inflation, is evidently absurd. Absurdity is visible also in the tortured and self-contradictory efforts made to explain policy choices, such as Chairman Powell's assertion in early 2022 that inflation, "a severe threat to the achievement of maximum employment," must be controlled—by increasing interest rates and thus provoking higher unemployment.[9]

What makes it so particularly difficult to make one's way through the thickets of professional economic writing on inflation—and deflation, for that matter—is not so much the inherent complication of the subject as, we shall see, the extremely peculiar treatment of money fundamental to mainstream economic theory. This is one among many oddities of economics as an attempt to analyze modern society. Another is the multiplicity of conflicting theoretical viewpoints—in the case of monetary theory, most strikingly divided between various modes of Keynesianism and Monetarism—something uncharacteristic of developed sciences. And another is the disregard of theoretical and empirical challenges to mainstream thinking, striking especially because of the field's record of explanatory and predictive failure. To give a minor example of this, 2021 saw a brief flurry of interest in a paper by Jeremy B. Rudd, staff economist for the Federal Reserve System, "Why Do We Think that Inflation Expectations Matter for Inflation? (And Should We?)." Examining the empirical and theoretical literature, Rudd shed convincing doubt on the conviction of economists and policymakers that people's expectations of future inflation are a key determinant of actual inflation. Observing that "Mainstream economics is replete with ideas that 'everyone knows' to be true, but that are actually arrant nonsense," he identified the role ascribed to inflation expectations—an idea central to official thinking—as one such.[10] The treatment of his article proved his point: despite many declarations of its innovative importance, professional discussion of inflation proceeded nonetheless on the basis of the analysis in terms of expectations Rudd had debunked.

This book is therefore addressed not, in the first place, to professional economists, but to the much larger group of people who, caught in the net of money, are affected in their daily lives by the workings of the economic system and may want to understand it. In a paper written for the National Bureau of Economic Research in 1996, economist (and future Nobel laureate) Robert Schiller asked, "Why do people dislike inflation?" Among the subjects who responded to the survey that provided his research materials, the "most striking differences ... were between economists and non-economists," whose "largest concern with inflation appears to be that it lowers people's standard of living." Schiller speculated that most people "seem to fail to think of the models that come naturally to economists about the competitive pressures that shape their wages and salaries; they tend to see any feedback on wages and salaries as working through the goodwill (or lack thereof) of their employer."[11] An economist himself, Schiller took for granted that the theoretical models provide a clearer path to understanding of the matter than non-specialists' everyday experiences. As we have seen, this is a dubious proposition. To understand inflation, and governments' attempts to control it, we shall have to construct an understanding of the economy that, while attending to economists' theorizing, does justice to the puzzling facts of life.

1

Money, Goods, and Prices

What things cost is naturally of interest to those who wish to sell them and to those who want to buy them to satisfy some need or desire. For much of human history, of course, most people did not acquire what they consumed in this way; instead, they hunted, gathered, or farmed; made their own tools and clothes; cooked their own food. If they were high in a social hierarchy, other people did these things for them: they took a part of the social product by traditional right or by force. If they were in a community of equals, they shared. In the early modern period, however, at least in Europe, price fluctuations took on general social importance as more and more goods came to move from producers to consumers through markets. When the price of wheat was high, hunger loomed for many; when it fell, consumption increased and population with it.

In his great work on the origins of capitalism Fernand Braudel points out that changing price levels, visible already in data from the fifteenth, sixteenth, and seventeenth centuries, demonstrate the existence of "a network of markets in Europe" at this time, "the more so since such variations occur at very much the same time across a broad area." In fact, he emphasizes, "these prices that rise and fall in unison provide us with the most convincing evidence of the coherence of the world-economy penetrated by monetary exchange and developing under the already directive hand of capitalism" during those centuries.[1] By "world-economy" Braudel means "an economically autonomous section of the planet able to provide for most of its own needs, a section to which its internal links and exchanges give a certain organic unity."[2] He identifies early modern world-economies in Africa, the Islamic world, and Asia as well as Europe, which came to cast "a mighty shadow" over the rest of the world.[3] By the first quarter of the twenty-first century, Europeans had long since fallen under the same shadow as the rest of humankind; the planet as a whole was well on the way to being a world-economy, in which price movements in, say, the United States or China had serious consequences in both areas and nearly everywhere else.

The "network of markets" is woven by the movement of money from one place to another. Money travels, with the direction reversed, as goods move. But money also moves on its own, seeking investment opportunities. The value of money—what it can buy—is important to those who buy and sell goods, but also to investors, who want to make money that will continue to have at least its original value. It was therefore of concern to those—the originators of economic science—who tried to understand the new social system of capitalism as it was emerging. Seventeenth-century economists—the so-called Mercantilists— identified wealth with money, and theorized the importance of government policies to maximize national money income. By the later eighteenth century, a distinction had been drawn between the "value" of goods, now identified as the real "wealth of nations," and its representation by money price. According to Adam Smith, writing in 1776, the value of a good is determined by the effort required to produce it; goods exchange in quantities set approximately by their relative labor contents; price is measured by the amount of the money commodity—by this time in Europe normally a precious metal—whose value equates to that of the good for which it is exchanged. It followed from this that, while prices represent values, they can change (like pictures of different sizes representing the same object) while values remain the same. As the productivity of the labor required to mine and refine gold or silver increases or decreases, the relative values of quantities of traded commodities and metallic currency units alter. Both changes in commodity values and changes in the value of money produce changes in prices.

In contemporary economics, the labor theory of value Smith shared with other writers of his time has long been discarded. But economists still think of the market economy, as Smith did, as a highly complex barter system, in which the owners of goods exchange them for each other. This is the "real economy," so called because today's economists still accept Smith's assumption that the consumption of goods is "the sole end and purpose of all production." For economic theory since the eighteenth century, in a society of free individuals (not subject, for instance as slaves or serfs, to some ruling authority) self-interest motivates them to meet each other's various needs by mutually exchanging the different kinds of things they make. Entrepreneurial types organize the production process as efficiently as possible in return for a share of the proceeds from market exchange; it is their wish to gain this profit that, as they compete with each other for buyers, drives increasing productivity and the expansion of social wealth. In this picture of the economy, money plays the role of a technical means for facilitating the complex web of exchanges.

Value in the "real" economy can be expressed, from this theoretical viewpoint, as a relation between two exchangeable goods, each of which measures the value of the other. Depending on the theory of value employed—economists differ on this— this relation may be explained in terms of the amounts of "utility"—psychological satisfaction—each good has for each of the exchangers, or as measured by the preference each has for one good over others. The relative value of goods is set when the supply and demand for each good match. Prices are just the money names of "real" values, the amounts of some standard monetary unit for which goods are exchangeable. Over time, as tastes change, methods of production alter, and random events (like wars or weather) impinge on the economy, prices and quantities will—in theory—adjust until supply and demand are once again in harmony.

The value of money—measured by the quantity of goods it can buy—is thought by practitioners of the "neoclassical" economics that has been central to mainstream doctrine since the later nineteenth century to be determined by its own supply and demand conditions. According to this idea, if there is a lot of money relative to other goods, its value will go down, and vice versa. These changes in the value of money appear as changes in the prices regulating the market economy. They can rise, on average (inflation), or fall (deflation). Because price changes can affect economic decision-making, forces determining the supply of and demand for money can act on the "real" economy, distorting its self-regulation in the short run, though over a long enough time equilibrium will be re-established. John Maynard Keynes, although working within the neoclassical framework, argued that strictly monetary considerations—in particular the rate of interest on money borrowed for investment purposes and people's reluctance to spend money because of uncertainty about the future—can shape the conditions of price-determining equilibrium, making the "short run" uncomfortably long. (And anyway, he observed, "in the long run we are all dead.") He and his followers believed that this made it both necessary and possible for governments to interfere with the economic machinery in ways that would maximize social well-being, without worrying over-much about inflationary effects.

Apart from theories, something like the relation between the value and price of goods appears within money itself. It has long been noticed that metallic coins in use were devalued by the alteration of their metallic content but still served as means of payment for goods. Rulers watered down silver coins with cheaper metals; merchants as well as rulers physically "clipped" coins as they passed through their hands, accumulating the clippings for their value. Indeed, the mere handling of coins wore away their material, reducing their commodity value even while their official face value remained the same. The difference between money as a representation of value and its actual value as a piece of metal was recognized in the phenomenon that came to be known as Gresham's Law, that "bad money drives out good": full-value coins will vanish from circulation, hoarded as material wealth, while their place in commerce is taken by relatively symbolic money. Thomas Gresham, a financial counselor to Queen Elizabeth I of England, advised her that as a result of the "Great Debasement" of the currency by Henry VIII, who had increased his treasury's (nominal) holdings without raising taxes by replacing 40 percent of the silver content of the currency by base metals, "all your fine gold was convayed out of this your realm," leaving devalued silver coins to do the work of money. This fall in the commodity value of the currency gave rise to an enormous inflation of prices within England, as it took more coins of a given denomination to make up a certain sum of value, and a deterioration of the exchange rate of English money in the Antwerp cloth market, crucial for England as a major exporter of woolens.

Elizabeth took Gresham's advice. Her treasury fixed the value of the pound at four ounces of silver; all coins in circulation were called in and the metal reminted. Despite episodic instability, "the pound sterling, having been stabilized in 1560–1 by Elizabeth 1 . . . [maintained] its intrinsic value until 1920 or indeed 1931."[4] Interestingly, while at the end of the sixteenth century the recoinage led to increased earnings for British exporters, it had little effect on the domestic price level. Already at this time the relation between the value of money and the level of prices was not as straightforward as might be thought. And, as Braudel suggests, the stability of the pound over time was due at least as much to Britain's economic success as to any monetary manipulations. In return, the fixed currency made possible confidence in contracts and so easy credit, since loans would be repaid at their full value, including those loans made to the monarch, strengthening the economy.

In the later seventeenth century English silver coins were once more clipped and worn down, losing up to 50 percent of their content. At this time, as Gresham's Law again drove silver out of the marketplace, gold replaced silver as the commodity basis of the British money system when the system was stabilized again thanks to a reminting overseen by Isaac Newton. Even a major economic crisis at the century's end, provoked by bad harvests as well as the expenses of war against France, was successfully overcome and the national money fixed in value. By this time, as we shall see below, metal was being replaced by paper, raising the problem of the value of money in a different way.

As Karl Marx explained in his discussion of money in the first volume of *Capital*, "The fact that the circulation of money itself splits the nominal content of coins away from their real content, dividing their metallic existence from their functional existence, this fact implies the latent possibility of replacing metallic money with tokens made of some other material, i.e. symbols which would perform the function of coins."[5] Paper money certainly represents a saving of material and a gain in convenience. But what determines the value of purely symbolic money—and how does it affect the level of prices stated in terms of it? Experience over time suggested both that paper money could maintain its value and that it could also give rise to disruptive inflation.

Paper

Government-issued paper money—now generally termed "fiat" money—had been used to replace metal coins in China since the seventh century AD; visiting in the thirteenth century (Yuan Dynasty), Marco Polo observed that "wheresoever a person may go throughout the Great Khan's dominions he shall find these pieces of paper current, and shall be able to transact all sales and purchases of goods by means of them just as well as if they were coins of pure gold." This was not quite true: use of the paper currency was restricted in area and time, probably in an effort not to repeat the inflationary experiences that accompanied the use of such currency in the previous Song Dynasty.[6]

In Europe, a different form of paper money emerged from banking practices in the late Middle Ages and Renaissance. As a market economy began to emerge from the complex development of late feudalism, when land-owning lords explored new methods to extract surplus product from serfs and peasants, trade expanded within Europe and beyond. Money moved from one merchant to another and from one place to another in the form of "bills of exchange"—IOUs—issued by a banker for payment by another banker in a different city. In this way, a traveling merchant did not have to carry quantities of precious metal with him, and business could be transacted across areas utilizing different local currencies. Currencies were mutually translated by their joint equation to an imaginary "money of account," another mode of differentiation of monetary substance and function. (The bankers at both ends charged for the service.) As the use of such bills expanded, merchants could use them to settle accounts; eventually they began to circulate as themselves a form of currency. In principle they could always be redeemed for metallic coins ("specie"), but it was more convenient to skip this step.

Banks store people's money and lend it out to other people (paying interest to the former and charging interest to the latter). Since money lent is due to be returned, it can be represented by a claim for payment on the bank—a banknote. Since not everyone reclaims the money they've deposited at the same time, and the money lent by banks is returned at different times, the same money can be loaned to more than one borrower: the bank attempts to keep enough money in reserve to pay out whatever claims are likely over time. The money can be loaned as a note—another form of IOU—or in the form of a new deposit, in the borrower's name, in the loaning bank; thus the original money lent to the bank can appear in two or more different deposits, each of which can be used to make payments by banknote. In this way, as with bills of exchange, banks enlarge the supply of money.

This system took on a new dimension with the foundation of national banks—the ancestors of today's central banks—originally created to lend money to the state. Government borrowing from wealthy merchants and bankers, especially to meet expenses of war, was a common feature of early modern aristocratic states and republics, notably in Florence, Venice, and Genoa. As nation-states developed out of the earlier decentralized system of city-states and aristocratically ruled territories, tension developed between the rulers' growing need for funds and the demand of the rising monied class for eventual repayment, and for money that kept its value between loan and repayment.

Much of the conflict between King Charles I of England and Parliament that led to the English Civil Wars concerned the funding of royal affairs. When the Glorious Revolution of 1688 led to the installation of the Dutch King William III on the English throne, finances were an important aspect of the settlement between Parliament and the new king. As Geoffrey Ingham summarizes:

> William was intentionally provided with insufficient revenues for normal expenditures and, consequently, was forced to accept dependence on Parliament for additional funds. Second ... the government adopted long-term borrowing [against] specific tax revenues for the interest payments.[7]

The settlement established the principle—over time generalized from England to all modern states—of the subordination of the state to the interests of private property owners. While the state has its own interests, provoking many instances of conflict between the two, it must ultimately serve the "money power," as it came to be called, for that is the source of its financial resources.

With England at war with France in 1690, William needed a vast amount of funds to build a navy, among other military purposes. A group of subscribers were induced to put together the sum of £1.2 million, loaned to the royal treasury at 8 percent, along with a service charge of £4,000 a year. Incorporated as the Governor and Company of the Bank of England, the enterprise was authorized to take deposits, deal in bills of exchange, and issue banknotes, with the loan as collateral, which they could then lend out. The bank earned interest both on its loan to the government (repaid out of taxes and new loans) and by lending to private borrowers.

In this way paper money became interchangeable with the metallic money issued by the royal treasury. In principle, banknotes represented gold on deposit at a bank, for which they could be at any time redeemed. But in fact such redemption was not called for in the normal course of commercial events. This was made clear, paradoxically, by a breakdown in normality, when the Bank of England suspended the convertibility of its notes— the right to exchange them for gold—between 1797 and 1821, during another major struggle with France, the wars against the Revolution and then Napoleon's empire. A collapse in the value of the *assignats*, the paper currency issued by the revolutionary government in France, led French holders of claims in pounds to collect, moving gold out of England. When French military successes in 1797 triggered English bank runs, many local banks were drained of their gold reserves, and had to borrow from the

Bank of England. The suspension of convertibility allowed monetary gold to move between England and other countries while the domestic economy was transacted in paper.

By the time Napoleon was defeated in 1815, the price level in Britain was over 22 percent higher than it had been in 1797. Was this inflation caused by the use of an inconvertible paper money, which could be printed in quantities determined by the treasury and the Bank of England rather than in accordance with gold bullion in the bank? This question gave rise to a debate about the causes of inflation, in which David Ricardo, the most important British economist after Smith, took the position that the free issue of banknotes to buy government debt and pay for war, enlarging the supply of money relative to the actual production of goods, had led to the increase in prices. Parliament established a Bullion Committee to study the issue, and it concluded that the so-called bullionist side of the argument—the idea that the money supply must be kept in line with the actual quantity of commodity money, gold bullion, in the system in order to prevent excess money from distorting prices—was correct.

The argument was resumed after the return to convertibility in 1821. The so-called Currency School of economists and parliamentarians insisted that a working gold standard required that the issue of banknotes, in the existing mix of metallic and paper currency, expand and contract one-to-one with actual gold reserves—a stricter requirement than simple convertibility. A leading member of the opposing "Banking School," the successful financier and economist Thomas Tooke, though originally a bullionist, changed his position after years of statistical research and analysis culminating in a six-volume *History of Prices* (1838–57). Tooke argued that price rises and falls were an aspect of systemwide economic movements, and that the inflation of the early 1800s was due to bad harvests, the disruption of the economy by war, and the blockade imposed by France on English trade, among other phenomena. As in the earlier debate, the bullionist side won, and the Bank Act of 1844 imposed the limit on note issuance demanded by the Currency School.

Two hundred years later, the argument about the causes of the inflationary burst in early 2021—was it due to excess demand provoked by too great a money supply or to conjunctural features of world trade?—was at base the same as these nineteenth-century debates.

Inflation

The idea that inflation is caused by an excessive issue of paper notes had been reinforced in the eighteenth century by a few brief experiences with a pure paper currency. The *assignats* already mentioned had been issued by the French revolutionary government, starting in 1789, with a promise that they would be redeemed within five years for coin earned by the sale of lands seized from the Church and the king.[8] While at first land was sold and *assignats* redeemed, as the wars against the European enemies of the revolution proceeded more and more *assignats* were printed to pay for troops and supplies. The increasing quantity of paper—45 billion livres' worth had been issued by 1796, against land valued at 3 billion—lost its value and prices shot up. Finally, the exchange of what became a nearly worthless currency against land was halted and creditors were legally protected from repayment in *assignats*. In 1797, the government of the Directory returned to gold and silver money.

As political economist Robert Skidelsky observes, what can be viewed as a lesson in the inflationary consequences of over-issued currency was also, from another point of view, a great success: "the government obtained its finance, speculators bought up the confiscated property at rock-bottom prices, and the real income of everyone else suffered a catastrophic fall."⁹ The inflation, that is, served to transfer wealth from the population at large to the government and land speculators.

Paper money had earlier played a central role in the American Revolution, with similar inflationary effects. The Continental Congress issued notes to pay the expenses of the revolutionary war. This was true "fiat" money, dependent for its character as money (its universal exchangeability) on government edict. Congress urged the states to impose taxes for the ultimate redemption of these "bills of credit," but the state legislatures failed to do so. By late 1779, Congress had enlarged the production of "Continentals" forty-fold, and the states joined in, printing their own currencies. Especially given the limited production of goods in the postcolonial economy and limited imports to it, prices rose as freely as the money was printed and the money with which loans were repaid became nearly worthless. By 1781, a paper dollar was worth less than two cents in gold coin. In the words of J. K. Galbraith, "the United States came into existence on a full tide not of inflation but of hyper-inflation."¹⁰

What has been called the second American Revolution, the Civil War of 1861–5, brought a variation on the use of fiat money. The Union government had to meet the expenses of war with a tax base diminished by the secession of the southern states. President Lincoln did not want to borrow abroad, difficult in any case because both Great Britain and France favored the South.

Congress authorized new, federally chartered banks to issue United States Notes, a nonconvertible paper money backed by the credit of the banks as holders of government bonds (printed in green, the notes were called greenbacks) that could be used to buy those bonds as well as for most other purposes; their purchasing power rose and fell with military successes and failures. By 1864, the price of gold had risen by 200 percent of the 1861 price in greenbacks and the cost of living by about 170 percent; after this, money began to stabilize in value when it became clear that the North was going to win the war. The end of the war led to a great public debate, conducted in pamphlets and books, over the question of whether the country should continue using paper money or return to gold. American bullionists, comparing greenbacks to Continentals and *assignats*, stressed the danger of inflation, controllable by the natural value of gold. Greenbackers argued that "to have a permanent, uniform, government-run national banking system based on inconvertible currency at low interest rates," while in conflict with the interest of bankers and other creditors in the northeast, was in the interest of American farmers and working people.[11] In the end, the financiers won and gold convertibility was reinstated in 1878.

Wartime finance was also at the root of history's most famous hyperinflation, the spectacular fall to worthlessness of the German Reichsmark in the early 1920s. Not wishing to pay for the First World War by imposing an income tax on its upper classes, the Reich suspended convertibility to conserve its gold holdings and borrowed money to pay its bills. At the end of the war, with the economy in a bad state and unable to generate the funds needed to repay the loans, it followed the by now time-honored path of printing money to meet expenses. These were increased enormously when the victors in the war imposed massive reparations on Germany (ironically, the German government, assuming it would win, had intended to pay its debts by imposing reparations on the Allies). Reparations were required to be paid in gold or foreign currencies, as were debts to foreign creditors; thus the mark, already weakened by the size of the debt in relation to the economy, rapidly lost value in foreign-exchange markets and domestically as well. The exchange rate against the dollar, 4.2 at the end of the war, fell to 4.2 trillion by November 1923. The Reichsbank introduced a new currency, the Rentenmark, and monetary affairs were stabilized by 1924. As in the case of the *assignats*, the inflation succeeded in eliminating the government's war debt while aiding speculation—now on the stock market as well as commodities, instead of land— and transferring income from wage-earners and those on fixed incomes or with small savings to industrialists and bankers, who were able to buy up assets with depreciating money. According to the Italian economist Costantino Bresciani-Turroni, who observed the scene in various official capacities in Berlin during the inflation period,

> The social effects of the inflation in Germany were not substantially different from those which had occurred in the past whenever the circulating medium had depreciated, nor from those which during and after the World War were apparent, to a greater or lesser degree, in all countries with a depreciated currency . . . it may be said that on the whole the inflation generally favoured entrepreneurs and the owners of material means of production, especially strengthening the positions of industrial

capitalists; that it caused a lowering of the real wages of workmen; that it decimated or destroyed altogether the old middle class of investors . . .; and that it created a new middle class of intermediaries, traders, small speculators on the Bourse, and small profiteers from the monetary depreciation.[12]

The term "inflation" had entered the vocabulary of economics about halfway between the issue of the *assignats* and the rise of the German price of a loaf of bread to 200 billion marks in 1923; the earliest British use in the *Oxford English Dictionary* dates from 1864. An American book of 1855 noted "the astonishing proportion between the amount of paper circulation representing money, and the amount of specie actually in the Banks," complaining that this "inflation of the currency makes prices rise."[13] Here it is the quantity of paper currency that is inflated; later the term settled into its present-day meaning of an increase in prices. Eventually, "deflation" also made its appearance in economic usage, to signify a decrease in the general price level.

Such declines were, in the first place, noticed as following significant price level increases. For example, the end of the Napoleonic wars was followed in England by a sharp drop in consumer-goods prices between 1813 and the 1820s, after which they fluctuated in a narrow band for fifty years.[14] This collapse in prices accompanied the twenty years of depressed economic activity that came with peace, and it has not been uncommon for the two economic phenomena to be associated. It stands to reason that a decline in the economy should bring with it a fall in prices, as a suddenly over-large supply adjusts to a demand shrunk as wages are cut and workers fired, while slowing investment means a smaller market for raw materials and machinery. This is only the inverse of the fact that economic prosperity, with rising demand for goods and services, can be expected to push prices up. It does not follow, of course, that prices cannot fall without depression (any more than that they cannot rise without prosperity).

However, the long worldwide downturn that was first to bear the name of Great Depression, lasting from 1873 to 1896, did feature a strong downward trend in prices.[15] Some economists—following the reasoning by which inflation is held to be due to an oversupply of monetary metal—explained this event by the exhaustion of gold mines and the demonetization of silver as the world's industrial nations followed Britain's lead to the gold standard. Others pointed to the enormous increase at this time in the productivity of labor and the cheapening of transportation, with the building of railroads and the Suez Canal, as drivers of the decline in prices. The Great Depression of the 1930s, following on another period of prosperity and price increases, certainly also brought with it a serious bout of deflation, again blamed by some writers on faulty monetary policy, in this case government failure to increase the money supply as needed.

Since then, a new wrinkle has been added to the questions raised by large-scale price movements: the worldwide experience, since the 1940s, of more or less continuous inflation, often blamed on government fiscal and monetary policy. It was because of this experience that when governments responded to the Great Recession of 2008 by injecting huge quantities of money into the world's financial system, propping up failing banks and other businesses, many economists expected that the expansion of demand embodied in all that money would lead to high levels of inflation. When this threat failed to materialize, some economists speculated about the danger of a return to deflation, with an economy characterized by "secular stagnation," a Great Depression-era concept that made a comeback after former U.S. Treasury Secretary Lawrence Summers featured it in a speech in 2013. The rapid inflation of 2021, however, while confounding those concerned about deflation, confirmed the fears of those who had expected price rises all along. Whatever their theoretical views, nearly all economists joined in calling for monetary and fiscal tightening to push prices down. Summers himself by 2022 "cautioned that it would be unwise for the Federal Reserve to be dissuaded from continuing with its plans for aggressive interest-rate hikes" since failing "to follow through would mean 'stagflation,' with high inflation making an economic downturn all the worse."[16]

Capitalism has changed, even if questions about the nature of money and its place in economic life are at least as pressing today as they were two hundred years ago. It seems clear that understanding contemporary inflation will require a look at the economic history of the last century, with an eye both to novelties and to continuities.

2

The Age of Inflation

Economic historians agree that the period around the Second World War marked a change in the history of inflation. From being an intermittent phenomenon, related to revolutions, government attempts to meet wartime expenses, and periods of economic prosperity, inflation became a seemingly permanent feature of the capitalist economy. In the United States, the Great Depression of the 1930s was, as was to be expected under circumstances of declining effective demand as well as increasing productivity, a period of falling prices. The enhancement of demand by government spending programs (the New Deal) brought a short-lived end to the deflation, which soon returned as the dominant economic note until 1941, when production for war brought a surge of inflation. This also, as we have seen, was to be expected. But not only did inflation persist into the immediate postwar years, but from then to the present—with the exceptions of 1949 and 1954, according to data from the American Bureau of Labor Statistics—the American economy has been officially in a state of inflation.

And this was not a peculiarly American phenomenon. From 1950 to 1973, the four largest European countries (Germany, France, Italy, and the UK) averaged 4 percent cost-of-living inflation; for 1973–89 the number rose to 8.4 percent.[1] Japan experienced a war-debt-fueled hyperinflation immediately after the war, reminiscent of the German experience of 1923, but the rebuilding of the economy after 1950 led to thirty years (until the late 1980s) of continuous inflation at what had become the normal scale for developed industrial economies. Speaking of the decades after 1960, when rising prices became an overriding preoccupation of economic policymakers around the world, historian Charles Maier observed that "the sustained worldwide inflation that began in the later 1960s did not reach the hyperinflationary proportions that rendered many currencies useless after World Wars I and II." Yet "the industrial economies had not previously experienced inflations of the combined magnitude and duration that the members of the Organization for Economic Cooperation and Development (OECD) suffered as a group" at this time.[2] Obviously, something new had entered the picture. But what?

Roots of the change have been identified in two major alterations in the economic system, at least with regard to the major economic powers. One was the end of the gold standard—the convertibility of paper money into gold coins or bullion at a guaranteed rate—as a link between national and international monetary affairs and as a regulator of monetary quantity.[3] The gold standard had been adopted by the major (and some minor) economic powers around 1870; the outbreak of the Great War brought it to an end in 1914. In addition to easing trade and capital movements among national economies with different currencies, it was associated, and often credited, with the *fin de siècle*'s economic growth and prosperity,[4] so efforts were made to revive it after the war. But the interwar gold standard was collapsing by 1931, as nations sacrificed foreign-exchange stability in efforts to deal with the national repercussions of the depression by easing credit, and was gone by 1936. Meanwhile, the standard itself had not prevented either the disintegration of the global money system in 1914 or the plunge into depression in 1929. (In fact, it has come to be held by influential voices that on the latter occasion an American monetary contraction—a deflation—was "propagated throughout the world by the international monetary standard," causing a global depression.[5]) By the 1920s, economist John Maynard Keynes, most famously, argued that its replacement by central-bank-controlled non-metallic money was essential to overcome depression and maintain prosperity.

In 1944, representatives of 44 nations—Keynes headed the British delegation—meeting under the aegis of the u.s. Treasury in the New Hampshire town of Bretton Woods constructed a new international economic system in preparation for the end of the war, instituting a "gold-exchange" standard. This was a system in which the u.s. dollar, itself internationally (though not domestically) convertible for gold, would serve as a monetary reserve (alongside and "as good as" gold) for all other national currencies. This system came to an end in 1971, when the Americans ended convertibility of the dollar, which had by then been issued in a quantity far outrunning their gold holdings. In the meantime, however, it had hardly served as a brake on non-stop inflation. In large part, as Robert O. Keohane points out, "The inflation that was accommodated by the international financial system in the late 1960s emanated from the United States."[6] Thanks both to the u.s. trade deficit and to the dollar's role as reserve currency, American money accumulated internationally, increasing the monetary bases of other countries without reducing that of the USA.

Today, the world's currencies consist of paper (or electronic) central bank credit money, backed in all countries by reserves of dollars and a few other currencies, and still—just in case—some gold. No position in economic theory dies, and there continue to be economists (among them, not so long ago, figures as important as longtime Federal Reserve System chairman Alan Greenspan and economist Jacques Rueff, an advisor to Charles de Gaulle) who insist that only a return to a true gold standard can overcome the plague of inflation, because only full convertibility restrains governments' ability to print money. But for all practical purposes, the gold standard is definitively gone.

The other major change since the early 1930s was the massive increase in government borrowing and spending that began with efforts to combat the depression, expanded with the coming of the Second World War, and has not stopped since. Taking these changes together, it is as if the twin phenomena of the early 1800s in Britain—the suspension of convertibility and the debt-financing of war—have been universalized and made permanent. Just as the bullionists blamed the British inflation of their time on the debt-facilitating disconnection of money from gold, so the postwar inflation came to be blamed on nearly continually unbalanced state budgets, facilitated by the absence of a metallic basis for money in domestic transactions, and in international ones since the end of the Bretton Woods mechanism. Nonetheless, while unbalanced budgets and "excessive" government spending were blamed for continuing inflation—its continual "creep" and its periodic flareups into double digits—governments and monetary authorities seemed powerless to arrest the trend.

Deficit Finance

A number of steps can be distinguished in this eighty-year process. In the United States, the New Deal, however carefully the Roosevelt government stepped, and however devoted it claimed to remain to the principle of a balanced federal budget, moved steadily in the direction of increased deficit spending. The government took an active role in the control of monetary affairs: the United States left the gold standard and devalued the currency by increasing the dollar price of gold, which both aided American exports and led to an inflow of gold into the country. The creation of the Federal Deposit Insurance Corporation, which guaranteed bank accounts up to a certain amount, stemmed the bank runs that were undermining the American banking system, while the creation of $3 billion in currency backed by government bonds replenished the banks' supplies of cash. Agricultural producers, ruined by the growing price differential between their produce and the products of manufacturing industry, were given government credits in return for curtailing production so as to maintain prices. As time passed and the depression continued, the government increased its spending to reduce unemployment and strengthen aggregate demand, borrowing more money to make this possible. Continuing fealty to balanced budgets led both to accounting shenanigans and promises that the balance would be achieved "next year," and to tax increases, including a major one in 1935. In fact, business conditions seemed to have improved in that year, but the downturn resumed in 1937, when private investment was still one-third below the level of 1929, and there were 10 million unemployed two years later.[7] Economists warned of "secular stagnation": the end of economic growth, brought by the "maturation" of the capitalist system.

To take the other major example of state efforts to overcome economic depression, German public works spending, under the Schleicher government in 1932 and the following year under Hitler, produced similarly meager results; though much touted by the Nazis, "the effect of the autobahn programme on unemployment was negligible."[8] The recovery of 1933–4 was powered neither by a revival of private investment nor by make-work projects and aid to farmers, but by a tremendous expansion of military spending. In the United States as well, something like full employment came only in 1941, when the armament and allied industries went into full swing even before the formal entry of the country into the war. In Germany, the prosecution of war on a scale beyond the material capacity of the country led to ever-expanding state control over the economy as well as the subordination of conquered European economies to German needs; in the United States the war "created full employment, deferred the prospect of secular stagnation, provided a respite from the controversies of the New Deal, involved businessmen in the management of government economic policy, and left behind an enormous federal debt, large budgets, and pay-as-you-go taxation."[9]

This situation, in its sharp contrast with the decade of depression, set the terms of postwar policy. Mass unemployment, while it had not radicalized the American working class, had clearly called into question the nature and future prospects of a social system in which an increasing majority of people are dependent on wage labor for their existence. Thinking of the market economy as ultimately serving consumption, it was natural for economists to frame the impoverishment of the suddenly wageless, along with the slowdown of business investment, as a problem of insufficient consumer demand, just as farmers and manufacturers experienced the economic contraction as a constriction of the markets for their goods, dramatized in falling prices. It was widely anticipated that the end of the war would bring a return of depression conditions; hence the idea that government, established as an economic actor by the New Deal and especially by its conduct of the war economy, should undertake the permanent assurance of full employment. The idea spread

that full employment was the important and essential means to deliver what every group wanted... Full employment became the first plank in programs to assist and adjust agriculture. It became the necessary condition... for reviving business profits and investment opportunities... It became the surest route to raising incomes of workers, not only by assuring them employment, but also by stimulating their training and upgrading.[10]

In the end, however, political and business fears of the possible social and economic consequences of unlimited promises of government support led to the transformation of the proposed Full Employment Bill into the Employment Bill of 1946, which called only for undefined "maximum" employment, along with the official employment of economists in a Council of Economic Advisers to the president. Nonetheless, it institutionalized the notion that governments were responsible for the maintenance of those in the wage-earning class whom the private economy was unable to use.

Hanging over American thinking about the role of government in the economy was, of course, the existence of the Soviet Union and, after 1949, the People's Republic of China, in which privately owned business was subordinated to a centrally regulated system run by party-states. Occupying a good deal of the world's territory and governing a large number of the world's people, these political-economic structures embodied the threat that the social dominance of private-property owners might be displaced by that of government bureaucrats. Paradoxically, limited state involvement in the economy was called for in the "free world" in order to preserve the "free market" in the face of what seemed at the time the onward march of a state-run mode of economy.

While the Bretton Woods agreements—which failed to integrate the USSR into an American-dominated system—laid a basis for the revival of international trade, its actualization depended on the revival of the war-devastated economies of Europe and Japan. Under the impulsion of the new Cold War with the USSR-dominated state-run economies and because it was obvious that the American economy could grow to capacity only as part of a revived global system, the United States supplied funds under the Marshall Plan to jumpstart a European revival. Japan's turn came later, as an aspect of U.S. government spending on the Korean War; Japan and Korea both benefited when the American military-industrial complex turned its attentions to Vietnam. In other words, the revival of the world economy now included the expansion of government economic action.[11] Already during the war, in 1941, the president of the Procter & Gamble Corporation said in a meeting with other American corporate executives, "The challenge that business will face when this war is over cannot be met by a laissez-faire philosophy or by uncontrolled forces of supply and demand."[12]

In Japan, for instance, the central bank made sure sufficient funds were available for corporate expansion while the government subsidized the large voting bloc of farmers (this was, in different forms and to different degrees, a policy of all industrialized areas) along with industrial corporations. In the United Kingdom, condemned to lower growth by the loss of its empire and its supplanting by the United States as the dominant trading and financial nation, public expenditure expanded and there was even a move towards the nationalization of areas of industry and finance. Italy also saw an extension of public ownership, of which, as Michele Salvati observes, "one of the driving forces was that of providing the party in office with a source of financial power and patronage that was independent of large industry and private capital."[13] In general, Europe saw the growth of welfare systems managing healthcare, retirement, and unemployment insurance, as well as half-hearted moves in the direction of state economic planning, such as recurrent Italian attempts to develop the south of the country. Both sorts of program expanded steadily in the United States as well, though there the largest portion of government funding went to warfare and preparation for it.

The end of the Second World War, following on a particularly deep and long depression, brought thirty years of prosperity. But even this Golden Age, as it came to be known (in France, *les trente glorieuses*), was punctuated by cyclical ups and downs. Economic policy now envisioned the task of maintaining high employment as one, in the words of Alvin Hansen, of creating "a balance wheel which can offset the fluctuations of private capital outlays."[14] The economists now swarming into government offices as advisors and civil servants had the idea that they could devise policies to maximize employment without creating uncomfortable levels of inflation. There was talk of ending the business cycle and "fine-tuning" the economy: according to leading economist and government advisor Paul Samuelson in 1955, "With proper fiscal and monetary policies, our economy can have full employment and whatever level of capital formation and growth it wants."[15] This regulation of business fluctuations would require the government to step in when necessary, using taxed or borrowed money. And in fact, "From the mid-1950s to the end of the 1970s, the share of public expenditure in the national income of the OECD countries as a whole rose by almost half."[16]

Increasing government expenditure, of course, carried the threat of increased taxation. Taxation lowers profits, so businessmen are always in favor of tax reductions, except in wartime or other moments of national emergency—and often even then. This principle came into conflict with the ideal of a balanced state budget, which itself expressed the idea that government activity should be limited to the minimum affordable with low tax rates. One alternative to taxation to meet government expenses, as we have seen, has been the printing of money, but by now this was expected to lead to untrammeled inflation. Hence Franklin D. Roosevelt, discussing government finance in 1934, distinguished between printing "greenbacks," to be avoided, and issuing money in limited quantities corresponding to existing government debt, giving currency the form of "non-interest-bearing five- and ten-dollar bonds" backed by money already borrowed and due to be paid back out of future taxes.[17] The other alternative, that is, is borrowing. Increasing debt, it turned out, was preferable to taxation.

In fact, once deficits became in practice if not programmatically accepted as the price of continued economic growth sufficient to achieve adequate employment levels, tax cutting emerged as the preferred alternative to spending. It began to be seen, as presidential economic advisor Herbert Stein put it, "that it was the deficit, not the spending, that did the trick" of avoiding recession, so that "the trick could be done by lower taxes as well as by higher spending." Both expanded effective demand, but the first did this without reducing the return on capital. This path was especially favored in the 1960s, when it began to seem that "the sluggishness of the economy since 1957 had been due to the poor prospects for profitable private investment, which had to be corrected by specific measures, notably tax reform, rather than by injection of more general purchasing power into the economy,"[18] especially because it was believed by many—especially in business—that high rates of corporate and individual taxation reduced the incentive to invest.

This preference was strengthened by the idea that, in the absence of adequate private investment, increasing purchasing power past a certain point produced inflation by strengthening aggregate demand beyond the economy's productive capacity, raising prices of the limited supply of goods. In the United States the recession of 1958, for instance, provoked a further increase in government borrowing and spending; as a result, it was held, the business contraction did not bring a decline in prices and the Consumer Price Index continued to rise. In fact, "The recession . . . seemed to be superimposed on a long-range trend of inflation which was then almost twenty years old."[19] Inflation replaced the unemployment brought by recessions as the central problem requiring solution by economic policy. By the 1970s the coexistence of the two had become such a regular phenomenon as to lead to the invention of the term "stagflation."

Fighting Inflation

Both business's dislike of government's increasing role in economic affairs and the related worries about inflation were of little avail in the face of the slowdown in profits observed in the late 1960s, which in both the United States and Europe led to a serious recession in 1973–5. In Angus Maddison's 1989 summary of economic developments,

> Since 1973, world growth has slowed dramatically. This is very clear in the OECD countries, where there was a sharp and widespread break in trend in 1974. It is true of the USSR and Eastern Europe. It was equally plain in Latin America, where the turning point came in the early 1980s. Except for Asia, the phenomenon has indeed been worldwide. In Africa and the Middle East there were even significant declines in per capita product after 1973.[20]

Though at the time it could seem like just another economic fluctuation, from the viewpoint of the fifty years of turmoil that followed—with bank failures, stock-market collapses, international financial crises, the onset of stagnation in Japan, and the Great Recession of 2008—it looks more like a major turning point in the history of capitalism. So, indeed, it appeared to Fernand Braudel in 1979: from his high perch overlooking capitalism's *longue durée* he wondered if, with "the beginning of our present difficulties, in 1972–4," we were not "embarking upon a much longer slide . . . a structural crisis which could then only be resolved by thorough-going structural demolition and reconstruction."[21] While it has not yet been resolved, it certainly marked the end of the postwar Golden Age.

The effects of this contraction were limited—and the resolution postponed, if Braudel is right—by even more government borrowing and spending. Public expenditure rose in Europe from 38 percent of GDP in 1967–9 to 46 percent in 1974–6; in Japan, from 19.3 percent of GDP in 1970 to 27.3 percent in 1975 and 32.2 percent in 1980; in the United States, which saw a decline of nearly 25 percent in industrial production between September 1974 and March 1975, spending increased from $264.8 billion in 1973 to $356.9 billion in 1975 (it had been $40.8 billion in 1950). The financial aspect of the crisis—in particular the 1974 failure of the multibillion-dollar Franklin National Bank—required action by the Federal Reserve System, providing freshly created credits as lender of last resort.[22]

Necessary though these measures were if the recession was not to have serious social consequences, they were accompanied by a rapid acceleration of price increases. The inflationary process that began in 1965–70 peaked in the 1970s and early 1980s. Not only Ronald Reagan, elected U.S. president in 1980, but a Committee to Fight Inflation grouping thirteen distinguished economists, including two top Federal Reserve System officials and five former Treasury Department secretaries, asserted (to use Reagan's words) "that inflation results from all that deficit spending."[23]

Inflation is particularly disliked by bankers, because it erodes the real rate of interest, since the nominal rate must be corrected for inflation, as well as the principal borrowed when it is repaid in devalued currency. Bondholders depend on stable monetary value to protect the value of their investments. And, like anything that raises costs, inflation makes life more difficult for people running businesses, who must strive to pass those costs onto other businesses and consumers by raising their own prices in the face of competition. While every business objects to increases in the prices of the goods and services it uses in its particular operations, all businesses can agree in opposing wage increases. The 1970s therefore saw much talk about "wage inflation" and a "wage–price spiral" driving inflation, which might only be stopped by curbing the power of unions to impose higher and higher wage settlements on employers. In general, as G. William Domhoff observes, "the corporate community was united in its opposition to unions . . . because defeating unions is the central power concern for the owners of all income-producing properties."[24] Fighting inflation provided a battle-cry for this concern, as well as for that of limiting budget deficits and potential tax increases by decreasing government spending on social programs and regulatory agencies.

It is hard for politicians to accomplish such tasks, limiting the effectiveness of fiscal measures to deal with the problem. Internationally, governments turned to monetary policy for help; one of the main arguments for the political independence of central banks is exactly their immunity to the pressure of voters—farmers dependent on subsidies, pensioners, trade unionists relying on government-administered labor law—to protect programs that aid them. In the United States, the man of the hour was Paul Volcker, appointed chairman of the Federal Reserve System by President Jimmy Carter but going into decisive action during the Reagan administration. The diagnosis—basically the old bullionist idea, ascribing inflation to an excessive money supply fueling excessive demand—suggested a solution requiring no legislative action (in fact Congress, following Reagan's wishes, was engaged in cutting taxes and thereby—especially as it was also increasing military spending—in massive deficit expansion at the very same moment). Instead, the Federal Reserve shifted its attention from directly setting interest rates to keeping the money supply at a target theoretically set by the ideal growth path of the economy. With less money available for banks to lend, interest rates rose. As Volcker's policy was explained by Charles Schultze, a Brookings Institution economist who had been the head of Carter's Council of Economic Advisors,

> In order to do what had to be done to stop and reverse inflation, the Fed had to jack interest rates up to unprecedented heights... the genius of what Volcker did, during the period when you had to get the public used to this, was to adopt a system which came to the same thing, but in which he said we are not raising interest rates, we are just setting a non-inflationary path for the money supply, and the markets are raising the interest rates. It enabled the Fed to do politically, during that transition period, what it couldn't have done in a more direct way.[25]

Inflation fell from 11 to 4 per cent between 1979 and 1982, at the cost of a severe recession, resulting in an unemployment rate of over 10 per cent by the end of 1982 and, two years later, the failure of 118 savings and loan banks and the bankruptcy of the Continental Illinois National Bank and Trust Company, the nation's seventh-largest bank. At the same time the Reagan government moved to limit labor union rights, lower unemployment payments, cut aid to poor families, and weaken industrial safety regulations and enforcement. Internationally, the rise in interest rates produced major crises for countries, such as Mexico, with large dollar-denominated loans.

In the United Kingdom Margaret Thatcher played the Reagan role of union-fighter, business-deregulator, and privatizer. Raising interest rates and cutting government spending, her government drove inflation from 17.8 to 4.3 per cent, with the expectable costs in bankruptcies, unemployment, severe damage to the national health system, and working-class impoverishment. Interestingly, when the French government of François Mitterrand, elected in 1981, attempted to move in the opposite direction by national-izing private companies and investing in public works and state enterprises, along with increasing the minimum wage, shortening the work week, and taxing wealth, it was rapidly forced to reverse course by capital flight and growing inflation.

Since 1973 "economic performance" has for the most part "deteriorated . . . decade by decade (with the exception of the second half of the 1990s)." This is not surprising, as "capital invest-ment on a world scale, and in every region except China, even including the east Asian [emerging economies] since the middle 1990s, has grown steadily weaker."[26] Only the Federal Reserve's easing of credit in the early 1990s stimulated the stock market and then a wild real-estate bubble.

> Seemingly, the Reagan years had opened onto a period in which state involvement in the economy could serve private enterprise rather than rival it: military spending subsidized corporate capital; the growing interest on state debt was paid to private banks while Treasury bills,

presumably proof against default, strengthened portfolios; and the easy credit facilitated by Alan Greenspan's Federal Reserve made possible a flourishing financial sector as well as the consumer spending that ultimately powered the whole world's economy.[27]

When the housing bubble collapsed in 2008, almost taking the world financial system with it, it was only a massive infusion of dollars into that system that arrested the development of a full-fledged depression. This meant the achievement of previously unknown levels of government debt in all the nations of the world—now including China, condemned by its new status as the world's second-largest economy to share the vicissitudes of global capitalism. As we have seen, this international rescue effort did not seem to produce much inflation as measured by the usual government statistical series (though prices soared on the stock, commodity, and real-estate markets). This perhaps encouraged the further gigantic fiscal and monetary stimulus with which governments met the business contraction occasioned by the COVID-19 pandemic. The return of inflation in 2021 brought a return swing of the pendulum—the re-emergence of inflation as the number one problem for policymakers and calls for the limitation of governmental economic stimulus along with worries about a possible wage–price spiral.

Were Reagan and the Committee to Fight Inflation right to blame governmental deficit financing for non-stop and over-high inflation? And if so, what mechanisms might connect the two? Two major mainstream theories have been advanced to explain the relations among government, the market economy, and monetary phenomena: J. M. Keynes's revision of early twentieth-century ("neoclassical") economic orthodoxy, which aimed both to explain the lengthy depression of the 1930s and to suggest ways to overcome it; and Monetarism, a return to a stricter neoclassical theory meant to diagnose the failure of Keynes's methods while explaining the ills they were intended to overcome. We turn, therefore, to a brief discussion of these two approaches to understanding the place of monetary affairs in a capitalist economy.

3

Theories and Policies

For centuries, the dominant conception of the disturbance of the economic system by monetary dynamics has been the Quantity Theory of Money, the idea that the general price level moves directly with the quantity of money, for a given state of the ("real") economy. This idea dates to the sixteenth century, when Martín de Azpilcueta attempted to explain rising grain prices in Europe as a reflex of the Spanish importation of silver and gold from the Americas, asserting that "money is worth more when and where it is scarce than when it is redundant."[1] This view was given greater currency, at about the same time, by the better-known Jean Bodin. In the eighteenth century a version of the Quantity Theory was espoused by, among others, the philosopher (and friend of Adam Smith) David Hume. Like the author of *The Wealth of Nations*, Hume argued against the Mercantilist equation of wealth with money. In reality, he said, "money is not, properly speaking, one of the subjects of commerce; but only the instrument which men have agreed upon to facilitate the exchange of one commodity for another."[2] As money is not wealth in itself but only a representation of real wealth—labor and commodities—"the prices of commodities are always proportioned to the plenty of money." Therefore, according to Hume, increasing the money supply by the creation of bank credit, though it may provide a short-term stimulus to production by increasing funds for purchases before prices have risen for most goods, in the long run, once all prices have risen, will leave the economy for the most part unchanged, except with a higher price level. Though Hume does not state it in so many words, his underlying assumption seems to be that whatever money exists in a given economic system will be thrown into commercial activity. A given supply of goods will rise in price as more money plays the role of medium of exchange.

As we saw earlier, the Quantity Theory was basic to the early nineteenth-century argument of the English bullionists that the depreciation of the pound following the 1797 suspension of convertibility was due to the over-issue of paper money by the Bank of England, and could be undone only by contraction of the issue. As Ricardo wrote, defending the conclusions of the Bullion Committee, "the addition of money to the circulation beyond the regular demands of commerce will diminish the value of that money."[3] Ricardo believed that "previously to the estab-lishment of banks the precious metals, employed as money, were necessarily distributed among the different countries of the world in the proportion that their trade and payments required," because trade would cause bullion to flow from less to more productive countries, where it was needed to facilitate a greater number of exchanges. Hence, if paper money was to be used, "the value of such paper must be regulated by the amount of coin of its bullion value, which would have circulated had there been no paper."[4] Otherwise, over-issue of bank money would produce a harmful disturbance of the national economy: the central bank's inflation of the currency, by raising domestic prices relative to foreign ones, would cause an adverse trade balance so that gold left the country. Hence, it was held by the Currency School of theorists, who took up the bullionist point of view when the debate revived following the return of England to the gold standard after the Napoleonic wars, fixed exchange rates, and therefore the security of the gold standard, required regulating the issue of banknotes by the quantity of the gold reserve. This principle was embodied in the Bank Charter Act of 1844, which aimed to counter the over-issue of credit money even under convertibility, which was possible because most paper was not exchanged for specie.

Equilibrium

The term "neoclassical" is arguably inappropriate for the products of the theoretical revolution in economics of the late nineteenth century particularly associated with the names of W. S. Jevons and Léon Walras, based as they were on abandonment of the classical approach to value (wealth) as formed in production, an approach concerned with the distribution of wealth among contending social classes. Instead, the new approach centered on the exchange of goods and services among individual owners, regulated by those individuals' subjective evaluations of owned and desired property. (Thus landowners were no longer a feudal leftover, whose demand for rent, by forcing up food prices and thereby wages, conflicted with capitalists' striving for profit, but possessors of a good on a par with labor services, money for investment, or indeed any other commodity, seeking exchanges like everyone else to maximize their satisfaction.)

Since each person's goal is maximal satisfaction, if no factors external to the "real economy" of production and consumption

—such as bad weather, pestilences, wars, or other sorts of government interference—disrupt its operations, it will settle over time into a state of equilibrium in which all individuals have made out as well as they can, given the resources at their disposal. Because consumption is the final goal of the system, and each individual chooses freely how to participate, abilities and wants—supply and demand—are adjusted to each other to maximize the satisfaction gained by society's total effort, thus harmonizing the welfare of each individual and that of society as a whole. Just because each individual seeks his or her own welfare, the system utilizes all available resources, including technology and workers seeking employment by entrepreneurs. Hence, unemployment is impossible. As Gottfried von Haberler pointed out in a 1937 study written for the League of Nations, only economic contractions—like the then-ongoing depression with its mass unemployment—needed to be accounted for theoretically, "since the upward movement, the approach to full employment, might be explained as a natural consequence of the inherent tendency of the economic system towards equilibrium."[5]

Equilibrium requires that the exchanges that hold the system together make mutual sense: wages must be set so as to make returns on capital possible when goods are sold at prices that consumers will pay. The central effort of the mathematical formulations of neoclassical theory (by Walras, Vilfredo Pareto, Gustav Cassel, Joseph Schumpeter, and others) was to demonstrate the possibility of a general equilibrium of supply and demand for all goods and services organized by the mutual relations of prices. The mathematics, taken over from the nineteenth-century physics of energy fields, was justified by the new portrayal of the economy as a mechanism, the system of simultaneous exchanges setting all prices, unified by the force of subjective choice.[6]

This approach, like classical theory, views money as an addition to the "real economy" of production and consumption, serving to facilitate the exchange of goods that constitutes it. As Joseph Schumpeter summarized this conception, for neoclassical economics

> monetary theory remained in one separate compartment and the "theory of value and distribution" in another. Prices (including rates of income) remained primarily exchange ratios, which money reduces to absolute figures without affecting anything except clothing them with a monetary garb. Or, in other words, the model of the economic process was in all essentials a barter model, the working of which inflations and deflations might disturb but which is logically complete and autonomous.[7]

There must be enough money to make possible the transfer of all goods from hand to hand; therefore the total amount of money, multiplied by the number of times each money unit is used in a transaction (the "velocity"), should equal the total number of transactions multiplied by the average price of goods. According to believers in the Quantity Theory, the quantity of money is the active element in this "equation of exchange": excess money will produce inflation; insufficient means of circulation will lead to deflation; both of these can have deleterious effects.

Thus the Quantity Theory was invoked to explain the fluctuations of business that had become disturbingly apparent since the early nineteenth century and which might seem to conflict with the theorized tendency towards systemic equilibrium. According to American monetary theorist Irving Fisher, writing in 1925, "changes in price level almost completely explain fluctuations in trade for the period 1915–23" in the USA and "dominate" fluctuations in trade between 1877 and 1914.[8] Such views have had a long life: as noted above, Ben Bernanke, chairman of the Federal Reserve System from 2006 to 2014, argued that the Great Depression of the 1930s itself was caused by a "monetary contraction" initiated by U.S. authorities and "propagated throughout the world by the international monetary standard."[9] Christina Romer, chief economic advisor to President Barack Obama, claimed to demonstrate that "nearly all the observed recovery of the U.S. economy prior to 1942 was due to monetary expansion," namely "a huge gold inflow in the mid- and late 1930s."[10]

Such ideas led in the period between the world wars to "attempts to overcome business cycles and stabilize the economy, the value of money, and world prices in a purely monetary way, by regulating the rate of interest charged by central banks,"[11] with the idea that this governs the amount of money banks can loan. Given the central role of credit in the capitalist economy, influential Swedish economist Knut Wicksell held that monetary institutions could regulate interest rates "in such a way as to maintain the international balance of payments in equilibrium and the general level of prices at a constant level." Similarly for R. G. Hawtrey, economic fluctuations "arise out of a contraction of credit across the globe" so that "if the flow of money could be stabilized," preventing such contractions, "the fluctuations in economic activity would disappear."[12]

Keynesianism: Rise and Fall

In the midst of the Great Depression, however, the idea of a naturally equilibrated system thrown momentarily out of whack by misjudgment on the part of the monetary authorities was less convincing. On the one hand, while increasing U.S. unemployment between 1929 and 1932 produced a steep decline in wage rates, this did not lead to the restoration of full-employment equilibrium. As John Maynard Keynes observed in his book of 1936, *The General Theory of Employment, Interest and Money*, it was "not very plausible to assert that unemployment in the United States in 1932 was due either to labour obstinately refusing to accept a reduction in money wages or to its obstinately demanding a real wage beyond what the productivity of the economic machine was capable of furnishing."[13] On the other hand, falling interest rates did not stimulate a satisfactory rate of increased capital investment. As we saw in the previous chapter, this state of affairs, in the United States and elsewhere, had obliged governments to act, not only by easing credit but by providing relief payments, price supports, make-work projects, and other forms of government spending. Ultimately it would lead to world war as a framework for reorganizing the global economy to make possible a renewed period of prosperity. Keynes's reformulation of neoclassical theory provided an explanation and justification of the expanded role of governments in this process.[14]

Keynes did not reject the idea that the capitalist economy tends naturally to an equilibrium of supply and demand. But he did not take this to mean that all goods would be successfully sold; instead he thought of equilibrium as a state of the economy with no tendency to change. He insisted that the determinants of both "supply" and "demand" require a closer inspection, and one more historically inflected, than they had customarily received. Economic growth, which brings increased employment, also brings increased income for society as a whole. Keynes believed—he offered no evidence but seemingly took it as common sense—that it was a fact of psychology that "when aggregate real income is increased aggregate consumption is increased, but not by so much as income." This disparity increases over time, due to what Keynes called a "declining propensity to consume." Hence the level of employment depends on the amount of investment spending: "there must be an amount of current investment sufficient to absorb the excess of total output over what the community chooses to consume." Accordingly, for a given level of demand, "the equilibrium level of employment . . . will depend on the amount of current investment."[15] And what determines this?

What is not spent on consumption is saved; it was taken for granted by neoclassical theory (which Keynes calls, confusingly, "classical" theory), for which money was simply a lubricant facilitating market exchange, that savings are borrowed by entrepreneurs, who pay interest for it, to invest the money in production. If business contracts, and more money is saved than is invested, this imbalance will bring the interest rate down, leading entrepreneurs to borrow more, and households to consume more. These changes will re-establish the equilibrium between savings and investment, returning the system to full employment.

This picture, Keynes contended, was incorrect. The rate of interest is not determined by the interplay of savings and the demand for investment funds, understood as the money representation of "real" consumption and production goods, but by the demand for and supply of money itself. Money has an economic reality of its own—Keynes's insistence on this was a major break with the neoclassical conception—because it is used not only to buy goods in real transactions but to speculate on future developments. People hold money—Keynes called this "liquidity preference"—as a hedge against the uncertainty of the future. "*For*," he stressed, "*the importance of money essentially flows from its being a link between the present and the future*," and thus a medium through which "changing views about the future are capable of influencing the present situation." If the mathematical general equilibrium of exchanges provides a static image of the capitalist economy, money makes possible a "theory of shifting equilibrium."[16] Whatever the long-run equilibrium promised by theory, in the short run a contraction suggests the wisdom of holding money to see how interest rates move, and with them bond and stock prices. Accordingly, a falling rate of interest can lead at once to increased saving and decreased investment. Such a situation—and in recognizing this Keynes again departed from orthodoxy—clearly limits the applicability of the Quantity Theory; only when all savings are invested, so that all income is spent either on consumption or on production, can the quantity of money even be thought to determine the general price level.

Money is invested in production with an eye to making more money, to collecting on what Keynes called the "marginal efficiency of capital," the expected yield (what the classical economists would have called "profit") of capital purchased at a given price. Keynes believed that the marginal efficiency of capital had to fall over time, as society's stock of capital grew relative to the demand for it.[17] To simplify his conclusion: the incentive to invest will decrease just as the need for more investment, and with it purchases of capital equipment, increases, due to the declining propensity to consume, if employment is not to shrink. As a result, "the economic system may find itself in stable equilibrium . . . at a level below full employment"—that is, in a long-lasting period of depression or stagnation.[18]

Keynes did not abandon the prime dogma of economics: "Consumption—to repeat the obvious—is the sole end and object of all economic activity." This is the ultimate reason why "Opportunities for employment are necessarily limited by the extent of aggregate demand."[19] But there is a conflict between the "real" economy and the monetary mechanism, which emerges to view in the phenomenon of liquidity preference: in the words of historian of economics Martha Campbell, for Keynes "the existence of money and financial assets allows for the divergence of individual and social interests" which are united in the "real" economy.[20] The dynamics of the market cannot overcome this conflict, and the effects of managing the money supply are limited. The Great Depression did not result from an inadequate money supply but from the collapse of investment in the face of declining demand. It follows, according to Keynes, that "the duty of ordering the current volume of investment cannot safely be left in private hands." The state must "stimulate the propensity to consume," directly "by redistributing incomes" or indirectly by government debt-financed employment-producing investment: "Pyramid-building, earthquakes, even wars may serve to increase wealth," though it would "be more sensible to build houses and the like."[21]

This did not mean, Keynes thought, that the market economy should be abandoned for a different way of organizing the production and distribution of goods. Though "the world

will not much longer tolerate the unemployment which . . . is
. . . inevitably associated with capitalistic individualism," he recognized "valuable human activities which require the motive of
money-making and the environment of private wealth ownership
for their full fruition."[22] The answer is what came to be called
the "mixed economy," in which government intervenes in the
private-property based economy only to shift the equilibrium
point towards full employment, without socializing private
enterprise or even competing with it. Finally, while accepting
the abstract principle of the Quantity Theory of Money, Keynes
argued that his proposals did not threaten uncontrolled inflation
because of the complexity of the interaction between different
economic factors. Ultimately, he concluded, "the long-run stability or instability of prices will depend" not directly on the size of
the money supply but "on the strength of the upward trend of the
wage-unit (or, more precisely, of the cost-unit) compared with
the rate of increase in the efficiency of the productive system."[23]
The money supply needs to accommodate both private investment
and government borrowing. But its management is secondary to
the management of demand by the enlargement and contraction
of government spending.

Keynes's work had an enormous impact on economic theory
and policy. On the one hand, although indeed "Marx anticipated
Keynes' criticism of the neo-classical theory through his own
criticism of classical theory," Marx's work was for all intents and
purposes unknown to most economists, who regarded it as an
offshoot of long-discredited classical political economy.[24] As
Robert Skidelsky notes, "Before Keynes, Marxism alone had a
theory of unemployment. So Keynes was overthrowing not only
existing classical [he means neoclassical] theory but the politics

of communism."[25] Keynes's theoretical innovations seemed a uniquely brilliant breakthrough out of an orthodoxy unable to deal satisfactorily with the capitalist economy of the twentieth century. Specifically, as Herbert Stein says, "the *General Theory* filled the need for an intellectually satisfying explanation of the total level of output and employment" in terms not basically alien to current economic thought.[26] On the other hand, it provided a theory that both justified the measures governments had already been taking in the face of the Great Depression and explained why they had not been sufficient to end the downturn: "The only error of the New Deal was its failure to spend enough."[27] The success of the war in producing full employment in the United States sealed the deal. In this way, even while embodying liberal opposition to the state-run system that emerged as an apparent alternative to capitalism after the First World War, Keynesianism justified the need for the increasing state intervention into the economy that seemed to have become a central feature of capitalism in the 1930s, and the social importance of the growing army of economists offering, beyond theoretical illumination, active guidance of economic affairs.

The Americanization of Keynesian theory—and as American economics, like American movies, became globally dominant as the country assumed its postwar position as the economic and military superpower of capitalism—largely dropped Keynes's disparagement of speculation while keeping his defense of the inequality of wealth. What became known as the "neoclassical synthesis" within academic economics effected a merger of Keynes's thinking with Walrasian theory, providing mathematical models into which data could be dropped to forecast and explain economic developments.[28] The growth of statistical information was a natural part of the emergence of massive administrative states claiming a science-based ability to stabilize both prices and unemployment while controlling the business cycle. But just as accurate forecasting proved harder in practice than in theory, the course of economic events as revealed statistically did not particularly confirm Keynesian theory:

> It might have appeared that whenever fiscal action was taken in an expansive direction the economy actually expanded in a significant degree simultaneously or after some regular period. But in fact no such regularity exists . . . Of course there are . . . cases which conform to the normal expectations . . . Eisenhower's drive for a budget surplus in 1959–60 was followed by a slowdown in the economy. Strong expansion of the economy went on after the 1964 tax cut . . . More generally, [however,] systematic comparison of the movement of the budget position and the movement of the economy in the same or succeeding period shows no systematic relationship even in direction.[29]

By the 1970s, with the end of the Golden Age and the reappearance of serious recession, Keynesianism lost its luster. In particular, the implications of Keynes's hypothetical linking of inflation with an upward trend of wages unmatched by the productivity of labor took on a worrisome aspect. In 1958, the inverse statistical correlation economist A. V. Phillips demonstrated to hold between money-wage increases and the unemployment rate suggested—since wages as basic costs are closely correlated with prices—that economies had a choice between price stability and unemployment.[30] In the course of the 1960s and '70s, not only did inflation rise to levels that business and governments found unpleasant but a "shift in the Phillips curve" allowed rising unemployment to coexist with rising prices, offering an opportunity for British Chancellor of the Exchequer Iain Macleod to coin the word "stagflation." It seemed that deficit spending, increasing aggregate demand and causing prices to increase, was not actually solving the unemployment problem. As Skidelsky, who has dedicated years to writing about Keynes, ruefully puts it, "Keynes was only partly right, and then only for thirty years."[31]

What if the pre-Keynesian neoclassical approach was correct after all? This had been held throughout the whole ascendancy of Keynesian theory by Austrian economists true to the original neoclassical vision; it was now taken up by an American, Milton Friedman, in a form popularized under the name of "Monetarism." What if capitalism really is self-equilibrating at a "natural" rate of unemployment, Friedman and his theoretical allies suggested, so that the attempt to lower joblessness below that rate would only cause inflation, further destabilizing the system?[32] The problem, this diagnosis suggested, lay with governments' creation of money for their own use in expanding demand. In other words, Friedman urged a return to the Quantity Theory of Money: "*Substantial inflation,*" he wrote, "*is a monetary phenomenon, almost always arising from more rapid increase in the quantity of money than in output.*"[33] Aimed against Keynesian prescriptions, fellow Monetarist Harry Johnson explains, the "modern quantity theory" differs from the earlier neoclassical version in "the assumption that disturbances originate primarily not in the instability of the private sector's behavior, either in spending or in cash-demanding behavior, but in the instability of the monetary authorities."[34]

Friedman bemoaned the effect of the Great Depression, which he preferred to call the "Great Contraction," in shattering "the long-held belief . . . that monetary forces were important elements in the cyclical process and that monetary policy was a potent instrument for promoting economic stability."[35] Rather than trying to manage the economy through fiscal maneuvers—which will not work in the long run anyway—the state should recognize that "the private sector will look after itself if left alone" and restrict itself to making sure that the money supply expands in sync with economic growth.[36] The post-Bretton Woods dollar, in actual practice unconstrained in quantity by any relation to gold, required some other principle to limit its quantity. Monetarism claimed to provide that principle and in 1979 Federal Reserve chairman Paul Volcker put it into practice.

Alarmed by increasing inflation, Volcker abandoned the Fed's earlier attempt to steer between inflation and unemployment by adjusting the interest rate for a policy of trying to keep the growth of the money supply constant. In this he was echoing Friedman's thought "that the effects of monetary policy may be expected to operate rather more than would otherwise be supposed through *the direct effects of changes in the stock of money on spending*, and rather less through indirect effects on rates of interest."[37] A central tenet of Friedman's was the idea that the money supply as a whole could be controlled by regulating the quantity of a core type of money, what he called "high-powered money." Also known as the monetary base, this is central bank-issued money: currency circulating though the economy plus that held by commercial banks in their institutions (for instance, inside ATM machines) and in their regional Federal Reserve banks. Since the Fed expands or contracts the money supply by setting the interest rate charged for reserves, in seeking to control what is called M1—currency plus checking deposits—Volcker's Fed was attempting to keep the expansion rate of high-powered money steady. (M2 adds savings accounts to the monetary total; M3 and M4 include even less liquid forms of money and "near-money," like certificates of deposit.)

Money and Government

The Federal Reserve puts money into the economic system when it purchases treasury bonds (and other securities) in what are called "open market" operations (it withdraws money from the system by selling Treasuries). It pays for them with Federal Reserve Notes—"liabilities" in accounting talk, IOUs against Fed-held securities, which can always be sold. It is these notes—government debt—that circulate through the economy as currency. In addition, banks can borrow dollars from the Fed at the "discount window" to maintain the legally mandated reserves that "back" the loans they make to businesses, individuals, and even countries. It is by setting the interest rates charged the banks (the "discount") and the quantity of open-market operations that the Fed influences the amount of currency in the system.

That all money is produced today by banks and other financial institutions tells us that the banking system, essential to the functioning of a capitalist economy, has acquired a governmental character. This is formally recognized by the regulation of privately owned banks by governmental or quasi-governmental central banks, and by such devices as government insurance of bank deposits. Even though today's dollar is a note issued by the Federal Reserve Bank, it is, as the phrase goes, "backed by the full faith and credit" of the United States government. Today's central banks are descendants of the Bank of England, which first fused bank credit with the sovereign's currency. Though I take the u.s. dollar, the world's reserve currency, as my example here, the same mechanism accounts for the euro, the yen, and all other national moneys. The role of central banks in regulating the money supply is thus an aspect of the growing role of governments in economic management.

Under these circumstances, even an anti-statist like Friedman could hardly call for the exit of government from economic regulation. What he did maintain, in a bold return to the Quantity Theory of the past, was that "monetary policy can prevent money itself from being a major source of economic disturbance."[38] Central banks should be unsung heroes of economic progress, keeping money in line with the economy's needs and otherwise getting out of the way. In fact, Volcker's attempt to put this idea into action did lead to a decline of inflation, but apart from that nothing went as Friedman had said it would. For one thing, the money supply turned out to be difficult to control, swelling and shrinking in response to the needs of businessmen and bankers. As Geoffrey Ingham summarizes, especially after the deregulation of finance promoted by the Reagan and Thatcher governments, during the 1980s

> credit instruments proliferated and were rendered more fungible and transferable into cash by the [deregulating] measures. For example, in both the usa and the uk, the hard and fast regulatory separation of deposit, or savings, accounts and current (cheque) accounts was relaxed, and the money supply was, consequently, augmented and increased ... The [Monetarist] policy became increasingly

inoperable. Later, in the early 1990s, as credit-money continued to expand at annual rates of over 25 per cent per year, but inflation fell quite markedly, the very foundations of quantity theory came under question.[39]

Meanwhile, the new monetary policy had its actual effects through the sharply rising interest rates caused by the Fed's attempt to restrict monetary growth. The economy, liberated from inflationary meddling, did not self-equilibrate but fell into a deep recession. In 1982, 66,000 American companies filed for bankruptcy, the highest number since 1929–32, and 24,900 went out of business, the worst level since 1933. Twenty million workers were unemployed, underemployed, or had given up looking for work.[40] Eventually, the financial system was seriously affected, with major bank failures.

Nor was the recession confined to the United States. Great Britain had instituted its own version of Monetarism, with a promise under the Thatcher government to use budget discipline to fight inflation with a decrease in the money stock. As in the USA, inflation did fall, at the cost of high unemployment and business failures. Meanwhile, the effects of the American experiment on what are called less developed countries with sizeable foreign debts, mostly in dollars, were devastating. By 1982, Mexico was facing national bankruptcy; default on its debts would have had an apocalyptic effect on the American banks from which it had borrowed. The U.S. Treasury and other government departments were forced to bail it out with billions of dollars. Within a year, this story was repeated for fourteen other poor nations. In the course of these events, Monetarism was abandoned as the basis for policy, with a return to flexible monetary growth targets and open fiddling with interest rates. In fact, the money supply was greatly eased and interest rates kept at historic lows for the decades that money managers liked to call the Great Moderation.

What is surprising is not the failure of Monetarism but the extent of the faith shown in it.[41] The Quantity Theory of Money had been an object of effective critique since its eighteenth-century formulation. The complexity of the interrelation of money with other economic phenomena has always worked against the pleasing simplicity of the theory, especially once the modern development of statistics made serious empirical investigation possible. While the connection between the inflow of American gold to Europe and sixteenth-century prices seemed obvious to Jean Bodin, twentieth-century studies, based on laboriously constructed data sets, leave most economic historians unimpressed by the theory's explanatory value.[42] Already in the mid-nineteenth century, Tooke's researches into price history led him to abandon bullionism. David Wells's book of 1890, largely devoted to examining the cause of what the late nineteenth century called the Great Depression, provided evidence for growth both in the gold supply and of credit instruments, so that the worldwide decline in prices must, he thought, be explained by "the great multiplication and cheapening of commodities through new conditions of production and distribution."[43] Near the end of that century, Wesley Mitchell's careful investigation of the greenback era in the USA also suggested the untenability of the Quantity Theory.[44]

Karl Marx's devastating critique of the Quantity Theory as espoused in classical political economy combined use of whatever statistical material was available at his time with a penetrating logical analysis of the arguments. Thus he found Hume's version of the theory to be based both on inadequate historical information and confused reasoning, notably the implication that "gold and silver have no intrinsic value and are indeed not real commodities" because "if gold and silver themselves have values," contrary to the Quantity Theory "only a definite quantity of gold and silver can circulate as the equivalent of a given aggregate value of commodities."[45] Marx saw Hume as led astray by his preoccupation with Mercantilism; similarly he took Ricardo's version of the theory and the bullionist position in the early 1800s to have been shaped by "the evolution of paper money in the eighteenth century," in particular by the experiences of Law's system, the depreciation of fiat money in the British colonies of North America before and during the revolution, and the French *assignats*. In Marx's opinion, "Most English writers of that period confuse the circulation of banknotes, which is determined by entirely different laws, with the circulation of value tokens or of government bonds which are legal tender"—that is, fiat money, which Marx thought could, under certain circumstances, present phenomena consistent with the Quantity Theory—"and, although they pretend to explain the phenomena of this forced currency by the laws of metallic currency, in reality they derive the laws of metallic currency from the phenomena of the former."[46]

Despite his great respect for Ricardo as an economist, he found that theorist's arguments both belied by statistics on money and prices and ultimately fallacious: Ricardo's proof that the prices of commodities depend on the amount of gold in circulation turns out to assume that "any quantity of the precious metal serving as money, regardless of its relation to its intrinsic value, must become a medium of circulation," that is, "this proof rests on disregarding all functions performed by money except its function as a medium of circulation," a conception earlier demolished by

Sir James Steuart (in an opinion accepted by Adam Smith).[47] In contrast, Tooke's researches—derived "not from some theory or other but from a scrupulous analysis of the history of commodity prices from 1793 to 1856"—demonstrated empirically "that the direct correlation between prices and the quantity of currency presupposed by [the Quantity] theory is purely imaginary."[48]

Fundamentally, Marx says in discussing the equation of exchange, the classical writers'

> illusion that it is . . . prices which are determined by the quantity of the circulating medium, and that the latter for its part depends on the amount of monetary material which happens to be present in a country, had its roots in the absurd hypothesis adopted by the original representatives of this view that commodities enter into the process of circulation without a price and money enters without a value and that, once they have entered circulation, an aliquot part of the medley of commodities is exchanged for an aliquot part of the heap of precious metals.[49]

In any case, Marx points out, normally bills are paid after the commodities purchased have already left the market, so that "the quantity of money in circulation no longer corresponds with the mass of commodities in circulation during a given period, such as a day."[50] This makes the Quantity Theory inoperable, an observation also made, in gentler terms, by Wesley Mitchell.

The mathematics of neoclassical theory were borrowed from physics, but not the historical involvement of the parent science with experiment-derived information. This is immediately apparent in the attempt to capture essential features of a continually changing system with a static analysis: as Morgenstern observed, "no amount of improved observations of a modern economy will have any bearing upon the Walrasian system which, using the inadequate conceptual-mathematical notion of maximization, describes only a hypothetical case of economic organization, far removed from reality however coarsely or finely described."[51] Thus in the course of explaining his own version of the Quantity Theory Irving Fisher, admitting that in reality periods of equilibrium are "the exception," as opposed to the more normal periods of transition between states of the economy, finds that the determination of the price level by the quantity of money holds only in the exceptional case.[52] According to Friedman, the "natural rate of unemployment"—the Monetarist replacement for the Phillips Curve—is "the level that would be ground out by the Walrasian system of general equilibrium equations, provided there is embedded in them the actual structural characteristics of the labor and commodity markets, including market imperfections, stochastic variability in demands and supplies, the cost of gathering information about job vacancies and labor availabilities, the costs of mobility, and so on."[53] But, apart from the fact that the general equilibrium equations cannot be solved for actual values, due to their immense number, numbers representing the "structural characteristics" mentioned exist no more than do numbers for the individual utilities or preferences central to those equations. And although, despite such problems, the theory in its Walrasian form was held by the Keynesian Samuelson and the Monetarist Friedman alike to have direct explanatory relevance to actual events, the links between the quantity of money and prices are so temporally and quantitatively vague in such uses as to make verification impossible. As one conscientious critic of Monetarism summarizes, "In no case of which I am aware has anyone succeeded in relating a demand increase [due to monetary expansion] with a price level increase in an exact, quantitative way."[54] Milton Friedman was sensitive to the problem of verification, and his magnum opus of 1983, *A Monetary History of the United States* (written with Anna J. Schwartz), enlists historical research in an extended argument for Monetarism. The key chapter is that on the Great Contraction, which aims to demonstrate that the Keynesian ideas that replaced monetary explanations of the Depression "are not valid inferences from experience." Friedman and Schwartz's own appeal to experience, however, consists solely in a demonstration that the Federal Reserve failed to expand the money supply as much as it could have after 1931, and the speculation that a more expansive policy might possibly have led to recovery. As the two authors themselves say, "Everything depends on how much is taken as given." They reach their conclusion, that Fed policy was responsible for the seriousness of the Depression, by leaving out of discussion "nonmonetary forces in the United States and monetary and nonmonetary forces in the rest of the world."[55]

The most important recent use of the Quantity Theory, to provide an explanation of the supposed generation of inflation by government deficit spending in the postwar period, has not stood up well to empirical research. For instance, a careful study of government spending and inflation in the OECD countries summarized its results as suggesting

> that the notion that deficits cause inflation—because they cause excessive increases in money which, in turn, cause price increases—is not generally true. In some nations,

such as the United States and Japan, budget deficits do not generate dramatic increases in money and the explanation of inflation must search either for nonfiscal sources of increases in money (as in the United States) or for sources of inflation other than increase of money (as in Japan). In other nations—for example, West Germany, where deficits appear to generate increases in money that are not, however, the primary source of increases in prices—the explanation of inflation must look to factors other than changes in the money supply, even if deficits are monetized. Thus, while there is support for strands of the monetarist hypothesis in several nations, it appears highly unlikely that the inflation experienced throughout the advanced capitalist world—and particularly in its three largest economies (the United States, Japan, and West Germany)—can be attributed to the budget deficits of government.[56]

Neither the theoretical and empirical weakness of the Quantity Theory nor the practical failures of Monetarism—like those of Keynesianism—have inhibited the continued role of both approaches as shapers of economic theory and policy. Indeed, the two currents have flowed together in the various schools of thought central to mainstream discussion since the 1980s. As Friedman, perhaps mellowed by his Nobel Prize, remarked in a reconsideration of the relation between the two approaches,

Keynes's stress on expectations has contributed to the rapid growth in the analysis of the role and formation of expectations in a variety of economic contexts. Conversely,

the revival of the quantity theory has led Keynesian economists to treat changes in the quantity of money as an
essential element in the analysis of short-term change.[57]

In the course of this theoretical rapprochement, as Ingham
comments, "orthodox monetary policy has become ever more
detached from orthodox monetary theory."[58] Instead, under
the influence of Rational Expectations Theory (an offshoot
of Friedmanism), attention came to be focused on economic
actors' "expectations," about future inflation and monetary policy
responding to it, held to be a determinant of the actual course of
inflation. Familiar problems reappear: in the words of a Federal
Reserve bank president, "While the theory is compelling, the
real world does not always cooperate." For instance, inflation
expectations "are not directly observable" but must be inferred
from a number of measures of the attitudes of different groups
of people. And in any case, the equations used in the studies "are
not able to answer the question whether high inflation leads to
increases in inflation expectations, or whether expectations of
high inflation affect household and business decisions, leading
to higher inflation, or both." Nonetheless, "policymakers need
to make decisions based on the available limited information."[59]

Despite the need of policymakers to make policy, Keynesian
theory turned out not to provide a path to permanent prosperity
and Monetarism did not find a way for capitalism to re-establish
its equilibrium. The eclectic mix of the two that has dominated
economic theory and policy since the mid-1980s similarly prevented neither the financial crisis of 2008 nor the recurrence of
conjoined stagnation and inflation in 2021. Amid the resulting
theoretical chaos, the period of low inflation despite the massive

expansion of the money supply in response to the Great Recession produced a revival of Chartalism, the doctrine that as a creation of the state money can be produced freely as needed for social purposes,[60] under the name of Modern Monetary Theory. In the words of a prominent contemporary representative of this view, government deficits are harmless, since "With a fiat currency, it's impossible for Uncle Sam to run out of money," so that as much can be printed as necessary to facilitate full employment. It is only when the latter has been achieved that "*any* additional spending (not just government spending) will be inflationary."[61] The return of high inflation led to an eclipse of this view as sudden as its rise to prominence had been.

Failing to control the actual course of events, economists no longer claim even to have more to offer in the way of analysis and prediction than guesses; monetary authorities follow the recipes in their repertoire without being able to make much of a case for their efficacy. Clearly, if the ongoing history of the economy is to be comprehended adequately, it must be in terms other than those structuring existing interpretations and policy prescriptions.

4

Modern Money

The failures of economic theory are not surprising when we acknowledge the obvious incongruities between ideas central to it and the realities of economic life. Apart from the dubious freedom of individuals it celebrates, most of whom must subordinate themselves to employers in order to survive, by the early nineteenth century the recurrent pattern of boom and bust now called the business cycle should have called into question the existence of a tendency towards equilibrium. Capitalism's history is one of continuous change, on a range of scales, marked by alternating periods of overall expansion and of contraction. From the early 1800s to the 1930s, in fact, capitalism was in depression between a third and a half of the time (depending on how such periods are dated, about which authorities disagree), occurring roughly every decade.[1] They became deeper, longer-lasting, and more internationally coordinated over time, culminating in the worldwide Great Depression that began in 1929 and ended only in the 1940s. As we have seen, though it was for a while believed that fiscal and monetary methods could tame the cycle, 1973 initiated a new period of economic turmoil, climaxing in the Great Recession of 2008 and the ongoing multi-year return of stagflation. Despite the terminology of "shocks" contemporary economics has adopted to explain breakdowns of the supposed equilibrium as due to unpredictable events impinging from outside the system on the smooth operation of the economic machinery, the regularity and systemic character of such breakdowns suggest endemic causes.

The bust periods of the cycle make particularly evident the fact that consumption, far from being the ultimate purpose of production, is subordinate to the entrepreneurial demand for profit: goods not profitably saleable are not produced or are even destroyed, like the food dumped to raise prices in the face of widespread hunger. Capitalists invest money in the hope of ending up with more money than they started with. Since investment is made in order to earn profits, and since the demand for labor (and so for goods consumed by the labor force) and production goods depends on investment, the ups and downs of the profit rate—the ratio of money earned to money invested—determine the well-being of the economy. This is why, as Wesley C. Mitchell pointed out, the business cycle came into existence in tandem with the money-centered business economy.[2]

In sum, money—far from being simply a technology serving the "real economy" of goods production and consumption, even if, as Keynes thought, it can introduce distortions into the proper functioning of the system—is essential to the way capitalism operates. As Mitchell emphasized, it is characteristic of capitalist society that "economic activities are . . . carried on mainly by making and spending money." He emphasizes that this is not the same as calling capitalism a market-exchange system: a "business society"—his preferred term—has not developed in any community until most of its economic activities have taken on the form of making and spending money. That way of organizing production, distribution, and consumption is the matter of importance—not the use of money as a medium of exchange.

This is why, for instance, so much of modern economic activity—such as insurance, real-estate speculation, or playing the stock market—is not primarily concerned with the production and consumption of goods. Most generally, in Mitchell's words, a business "is an organization which seeks to realize pecuniary profits upon an investment of capital, by a series of transactions concerned with the purchase and sale of goods in terms of money."[3]

As a result, not only are production and consumption organized differently today than in earlier forms of society, but money has acquired new features and forms. It is worth emphasizing this point, because money is an ancient social invention. But even though uses made of it in the past anticipated those of the present day—in ancient Rome, for instance, including profit-seeking investment, large-scale trading, and rudimentary banking—capitalism is the first form of society in which the reproduction of society as a whole depends on the use of money. In no earlier society did most goods move from production to consumption through exchange against money. Today, even the unmonetized work of home-makers (in 1927 Mitchell estimated that housewives formed "the largest occupation group, outnumbering farmers three to one"[4]) uses materials purchased in stores and premises bought or rented for money. The economists' distinction between "real" and "monetary" analysis reflects the idea that present-day society is at root no different from earlier social forms, with money simply adding efficiency to the operation of the eternal cycle of production for consumption.[5] In fact, however, it is a particularity of capitalism that the real processes of production and consumption depend for their continuity on the operation of the money system.

For one thing, "exchange" under modern conditions does not really mean the reciprocal transfer of goods between people. In fact, goods are for the most part directly exchanged not for each other but for money.[6] Such transfers are regulated not alone by the needs or desires of the exchangers—or, as in some earlier systems of goods exchange, by ideals of generosity or prestige—but by the "worth" or "value" of goods, as represented by particular amounts of money.[7] I choose to spend my money on a tin of anchovies; you may not share my taste. But whoever wants the strong-flavored little fish must pay the same price for them—their value, what they are worth. The price does not reflect my particular preference for anchovies; it is—to use Adam Smith's terminology—the exchange-value, as opposed to the use-value, of the salty delicacies. Money functions as "money of account" or "measure of value" in the price with which things are offered on the market. When actual money changes hands, functioning as "means of circulation" or—when delayed—as "means of payment," the value of those things has been separated from the use-values, which can now be consumed by the purchaser, leaving the value in the hands of the seller. This independent existence of the economic value of a good, materialized in money, is the counterpart of the fact that such goods are produced specifically to be sold to someone else rather than used by their producers. It makes possible the general movement of goods between producers and consumers by providing a tradable equivalent for the universe of goods. It is not a commodity possessed but the money gained by a sale, the value of the commodity sold, that measures the wealth of the seller: his or her claim on the universe of products.

Social production certainly does not require money-mediated exchange in order for goods to be circulated to their end users. Other societies use different methods to organize the movement of goods from producers to consumers. For one thing, the practice of producing goods for sale presupposes that the producers have the socially recognized right to do what they want with their goods. (In early twentieth-century southern African San society, by contrast, different parts of an animal killed by a hunter might already belong to specific relatives, such obligations binding together members of the group into a producing-and-consuming system.) This right is explicitly enshrined, in modern society, in the legal rules governing private property, enforced by the state; thus the development of the modern economic system required legal innovations to make possible, for instance, the buying and selling of land. On the other hand, while goods in the modern system are produced as the property of individual persons, they are for the most part intended to be consumed by others—in fact, by anyone who can pay what they are worth. Whether the effort made to produce them counts as part of social production is discovered only when they are successfully sold to consumers.

This was the aspect of "value" that the classical economists around 1800 explained by identifying it with the labor required to produce them. This idea recommended itself for a number of reasons: for one thing, it connected market exchange with the social division of labor, whose extension seemed such a key feature of the emerging modern society, explaining how a social system could be maintained by the actions of individual proprietors, each following his or her own interest. In this way it seemed to make sense of the exchange relation as a unifier of individual and general interests, the idea being that a person's contribution of labor to society gave that person the right to withdraw an equal amount of someone else's labor in the form of product. From this point of view, it was tied up with new ideas about the essential (legal) equality of persons; their ownership of their own physical capacities (hence there was already in the seventeenth century a conflicted attitude, visible in the writing of a social thinker like John Locke, towards the ancient practice of slavery); and opposition to claims to the social product made on the basis of status or tradition—the ownership of land, for instance, as opposed to undertaking the effort of farming it.

One problem with this "labor theory of value" approach, a problem stressed by Marx, was that because it treats the different kinds of labor producing different kinds of goods as directly comparable quantitatively—because "worth" amounts of the same thing, money—these kinds of labor seem to be samples of the same thing.[8] But "concrete" labor, as Marx called it, is differentiated by many features, including—beyond the differences in kinds of activity—such features as skill, danger, and prestige, which makes the comparison of quantities of labor either undefined or based on some contestable judgment. This helps to explain why until the advent of capitalist society words for "labor," the general category covering the variety of productive activities, did not exist in European languages.[9] Marx suggested that it is only the practice of exchanging goods for money that *makes* them mutually quantifiable; by giving each a monetary value—a price—we make them comparable *as values*, abstracting from their material differences.

In Geoffrey Ingham's words, "Money accounting... is the means of translating the work of the barber into that of the farmer," and thereby producing (or, as the contemporary academic phrase has it, socially constructing) an abstract version of labor.[10] The abstraction is not just conceptual (as when "animal" includes beetles along with sparrows): the *practice* of exchanging goods for money, which transfers ownership from one person to another, produces not just a set of relations between exchangers but a set of relations between producers and consumers, since the goods are produced specifically to be exchanged. In order for this to happen, money must be more than a mere symbol of the idea of "labor in general." It is the possession of money itself that gives access to the world of commodities—even if money is a piece of paper. Thus "money puts social power as a thing into the hands of the private person."[11] At the same time, the social quality of productive activity is obscured by the ascription of value to commodities. The price of a loaf of bread does not explicitly represent the relationship between the bakery worker and those who will break bread together. Yet it is the exchange of money for bread that links the two, as we can remember when we consider the system of production and exchange as a whole, in which goods are produced as values to be realized in money.

But what accounts for this historically unique system of organizing social production and consumption? Why invent a material representation of social labor in the first place? Part of the answer is the individual, private character of production, which is carried on without prior consultation with the possible consumers, so that it is exchangeability for money that carries the social character of the production process. Another part of the explanation—social-historically connected to the first—starts with the fact that the "persons" who produce goods are for the most part not the people who physically make things but employers of the latter; typically, today, legal persons, companies that are juridical producers and therefore owners of the product. This is hardly the first society in which people performed work for others: throughout most of history a portion of society's labor and product was by custom—by right—due to the representatives of the gods, to the state, to parents, or to the lord of the local domain. (Of course, the slave's output belonged to the master, apart from the slave's own consumption.) But it is the first social system in which control over working time and output is structured by the circulation of money.

Before capitalism, all over the world, people produced both the goods they consumed and those that were taken from them by lords and masters of various sorts, thanks to everyday access to land, tools, and other resources. Under these circumstances, monetary exchange could only be a minor part of economic life. It was the multi-century process by which in Europe agricultural producers—the vast majority of the population, with various traditional rights and duties to use of land and other means of production—were either driven off the land or converted into rent-paying tenants that laid the basis for the emergence of the business economy. Subsistence production was increasingly transformed into production of raw materials for manufacturers employing newly landless people as wage laborers to turn into saleable products. Towns and cities grew as centers of manufacture and commerce. As merchants expanded their operations to finance production, and the moneylenders who had serviced medieval merchants and nobles turned into bankers organizing the flow of money into investment in production for the market, money became capital, investment in business conducted with the goal of achieving monetary profit. By the sixteenth and seventeenth centuries, the system had expanded far beyond Europe, with the extraction of natural resources from the Americas, Africa, and Asia and the use of indentured servitude and then slavery (necessary in the absence of sufficient numbers of propertyless laborers) to produce goods for the rapidly expanding market system.

In the course of this process, money gradually became the primary form in which the fruits of productive labor were taken by landowners, who received as rents a portion of the profits made by farmers employing hired workers to produce crops for the expanding market. At the same time, the ability to labor—for eighteenth-century philosophers the basis of ownership claims to the product—became itself a good to be sold to employers who could combine it with the materials and tools necessary to set people to work. The transformation of different kinds of activity into "labor" by the equation of goods to money in markets went along with the transformation of landless laborers—once tied to specific pieces of land and traditional productive duties—into an abstract "labor force" available for whatever kind of work employers could invent.

With the emergence of this social arrangement, money, the medium of exchange, became a barrier between the producers and their product, the property of their employers: the employed workforce as a whole is required to work for money to purchase a portion of what they themselves have produced. Money is the form in which the value of goods needed by the labor force to reproduce itself is represented and in which the surplus produced beyond those goods moves into the hands of individual enterprises. For the most part, money earned by workers is fully spent on their reproduction (including reproduction of the class of workers as a whole by way of individual families) and very little can be accumulated. In contrast, the money expended by employers in financing production returns to them, with a surplus, when the goods produced are sold; consequently their position as proprietors and employers is reproduced, just as the position of workers as requiring employment to continue living is.

Since all income takes the form of money received in exchange for some good or service, the wage relationship between employers and employees—in fact central to capitalism as a system—appears as just one of many exchange relationships among legal equals. Paradoxically, the fact that the "real economy" itself is structured and regulated by monetary flows allows those flows to appear as an addendum to a system of exchanges between owners of things. In this way, the very centrality of money to the system makes it hard for those whose lives are structured in its terms to understand it—economists along with everybody else.

The Production of Money

Capitalism as it came into being made use of money as it existed in medieval society. Fernand Braudel has traced the broad contours of this development through such phenomena as the growth of periodical fairs at which merchants interacted with buyers; trade between European merchants and traders in spices and other goods in Asia; and the employment of mercenary armies by political entities in Italy and northern Europe.[12] The main materials of money were gold and silver, minted by governments into coins of standard weights and therefore values. As discussed in Chapter One, the very use of coins brought with it the degradation and devaluation of their metallic substance, giving them a tendency to function as symbols of themselves. While, as we have seen, this suggested the use of state-issued paper money symbolic of metallic coin, a more important substitute for commodity money came with the widespread circulation of banknotes, promises to pay that when associated with governmental or quasi-governmental institutions (the national or central banks) became "as good as gold," legal tender, payment in themselves.

Already by the mid-nineteenth century commodity money was showing itself to be inadequate to the needs of an economic system prone to wide movements of expansion and contraction. This lesson, inherent in the British suspension of convertibility to meet the financing demands of war, was not learned for more than half a century. The arguments of the bullionists, that the money supply should be limited by the gold holdings of the banking system, were enshrined in British prime minister Robert Peel's Bank Act of 1844. This law largely limited the power to issue notes to the Bank of England, whose notes were governed in quantity by its bullion holdings. The Act, like the earlier work of the Bullion Committee, was a response to price movements—in this case the collapse of prices that came with the commercial crises of 1825 and 1836—on the belief, backed by Ricardo's scientific authority, that both inflation and falling prices (and so commercial contractions) resulted from a disproportion between the quantity of money and the value of commodities in the market. The result, however, was a worsening of crisis conditions in 1847 and again in 1857, when the drain of gold abroad and the domestic hoarding of banknotes produced a shortfall of money that drove up interest rates. On both occasions, the government had to suspend the Bank Act to allow the money supply to expand to meet the needs of business.[13]

This experience was echoed after the First World War, when the re-establishment of the gold standard by the Bank of England required lower prices and higher interest rates that plunged the country into depression.[14] It was such phenomena that led Keynes to declare gold a "barbarous relic." While Keynes favored the invention of an international credit money (to be called "bancor") issued by a global central bank, the Bretton Woods agreement established a halfway house with its gold exchange standard in which the dollar served alongside the precious metal as an international reserve currency. Finally, after 1971, the world abandoned commodity money for a system based on central bank-issued credit money, still dominated by the dollar. Like the gold standard, the Bretton Woods system proved incompatible with the economic and political pressures of the postwar period, as international flows of capital came into conflict with national interests.[15]

An important feature differentiating bank-credit money from state-issued paper (the two are often confused, especially as the term "fiat money" is commonly applied to both) is the explicit foundation of the former on government debt. (This was the distinction that Roosevelt made in 1938 between printing greenbacks and issuing bills limited by state debt.) As experience recurrently demonstrated, inconvertible paper circulated by states normally operating with commodity money easily became over-issued as governments succumbed to the temptation to pay their bills by running the printing press. As Marx pointed out, metallic money in excess of that needed for commercial transactions leaves circulation and is hoarded, conserving its value (and undermining the Quantity Theory, which assumes that almost all money circulates). But paper money continuously injected into circulation will only lose its value relative to gold, other currencies, and the world of saleable goods. This is what happened to the French-Revolutionary *assignat*, issued far in excess of the land sales that were supposed to back it, and to the German mark when the government printed it at will to pay its war debts. Since in these situations paper was a symbol for the gold (or land valued in gold) which was still the official base of the monetary system, each of the increasing number of notes represented less and less of the money commodity and therefore had less and less value. It was this that made the Quantity Theory appear to be vindicated by these experiences. In contrast, central bank credit money, like today's U.S. dollar, is issued in quantities matching the purchase of government debt, in theory repayable out of future taxes.

This process can be hard to follow, because the dollar system seems to be a massive structure constructed in the middle of the air. (A Federal Reserve Note is an IOU of the central bank, but this debt can only be repaid with more Federal Reserve Notes.) Paradoxically, the producer of the dollar, the U.S. government, has no money of its own (apart from what it earns by, for instance, the lease of public lands). It raises funds to meet its expenses by taxation and by borrowing. Taxation is relatively straight-forward—the government by legal seizure extracts a portion of the money made in the private business system. Since the state depends for its existence on the business-based system, it will under normal circumstances limit its taking to a small portion of the money won in the course of the cycle of production for profitable sale; we can think of this, as businesspeople do, as a deduction from annual profits. Wages also are taxed, but if we think of wages as the amount of national income that the class of wage-earners will accept in return for their work, it is clear that

the amount taken as tax could just as well have been retained by
their employers.

Given the necessary limitation of taxes to an amount that does
not impinge on the ability of enterprises to remain in business,
when governments are in need of larger amounts of money they
borrow it from the private sector; in emergencies governments
borrow from other governments or international consortia of
governments like the International Monetary Fund. The treasury—the department managing government finances—following
the example of private businesses, borrows money by selling bonds.
These bonds pay interest; the price of the bond is determined as a
function of the security-market-wide interest rate. The collateral is
the taxes the state takes in, which—together with further borrowing—provide the funds from which the interest and, eventually,
the principal will supposedly be paid. Thus the basis of the monetary system as a whole—and this is true for the monetary system
of the world, in which the U.S. dollar serves as the chief reserve
currency—is U.S. government debt.

The value of that debt is sustained, first, by the sheer size of
the market for U.S. Treasury securities—in early 2020 there was
$17 trillion outstanding in Treasury debt—so that under normal
circumstances they can be sold without affecting the price.[16] This
in turn is due to the central role of the dollar in the global economy
as the reserve currency held by central banks around the world,
which reflects the dominance of the U.S. economy.[17] Ultimately,
it rests on the continued functioning of the world economy as
a whole.[18]

This is suggested immediately by the fact that central bank-
issued currency is actually a very small portion of what is normally
called money ("broad money"). These notes, produced by the U.S.

Bureau of Engraving and Printing, are issued to Federal Reserve Banks. From there they go to the commercial banks that are members of the Federal Reserve System. They are technically liabilities of the Federal Reserve—loans made by the member banks to the system. Their value is guaranteed by the financial assets pledged by the Federal Reserve banks as collateral—Treasury securities and federal mortgage agency securities purchased by the Federal system on the open market. Treasury securities, as just explained, are backed by collectable taxes; the mortgage securities are backed by the value of the mortgaged real estate, and in practical terms by the flow of mortgage payments. It is the flow of income to the federal government that provides the guarantee that Federal Reserve notes have value.

Most money (around 97 percent) takes the form of bank deposits corresponding to loans made by commercial banks to businesses and individuals.[19] By loaning money, as mentioned in Chapter One, banks create more money (by the same token, money is destroyed when a loan is repaid). Money is therefore constantly created (and destroyed) as businesses borrow money to buy raw materials, repaying the loans weeks or months later; households take out mortgages, repaid over decades; credit card bills expand and contract; governments borrow to meet expenses; and speculators borrow to buy assets for future sale (or use as collateral for further borrowing).

It is the continuous operation of a social system in which production and consumption are governed by the quest of businesses for monetary profit, so that the social character of production requires representation by the money price of goods, that gives substance to money as the form in which the value of commodities appears. The phrase Marx uses to discuss the origin of money in the course of development of the modern market system serves as well to describe the reality of money in the ongoing, developed capitalist economy: "Money necessarily crystallizes out of the process of exchange, in which different products of labor are in fact equated with each other, and thus converted into commodities."[20]

It was an illusion of pre-twentieth-century economists that money had to be a commodity. This was partly because of the idea that capitalism was a sort of barter economy, based on the exchange of goods and services between possessing individuals. From this point of view, money seemed to be simply the most exchangeable commodity.[21] Moreover, as we saw, the material reality of gold or silver seemed to guarantee the reality of monetary value, blocking the inflationary potential of the printing press. But, on the one hand, recurrent falls into inflation and suspensions of the gold standard demonstrated the incapacity of commodity money to safeguard the operation of the system under serious stress. And on the other, as Marx presciently saw, credit is capitalist money, particularly well suited to a dynamic economic system. Not only must the money supply contract and expand to meet the needs of circulation—thus, quite the reverse of the Quantity Theory, determined in quantity by the prices of the commodities exchanged at any time—but it must provide a vehicle for the pooling of monetary resources and the elaborations of finance, from bank credit through the stock market to the wilder forms of derivatives (financial contracts gambling on the value of underlying assets). Since gold and silver are "distinguished from other forms of wealth" only "as autonomous embodiments and expressions of the *social* character of wealth," it was only natural for credit, "being similarly a social form of wealth," to "[displace] money and [usurp] its position."[22]

Unlike commodity money, credit money has negligible value of its own. Its value is simply the things it can buy: it is determined by the prices of commodities. Since money constituted by state debt, as Duncan Foley observes, "is exchanged" just as commodity money was "against produced commodities," the value and so the quantity of money are constrained by these exchanges, as it is only an element—albeit one with a unique function and position—in the whole system.[23] Inflation—a general rise in the price level—is not therefore "a monetary phenomenon," but a product of the operation of the commodity production and exchange system as a whole.

Prices

The goal of capitalist employment, the eventual sale of a product for more than it cost to produce it, puts pressure on employers to pay no more for tools and raw materials than is necessary. The producers of those goods in turn must strive for efficiency in their production, since they pay for the time their employees spend on it, by reducing the time required to that allowed by cultural norms and the state of technology. The same is true for the producers of workers' consumption goods. And all employers strive to pay (on average) as low a wage as is compatible with a continuous supply of workers, something determined by the meeting-point of workers' expectations and the prices of the goods they consume. Finally, it is obvious—once you think about it—that, if we assume the average wage is sufficient to reproduce the labor force, the amount of time spent at work beyond the time required to produce goods equivalent in value to the wage, as represented as part of the cost of output, is the limit of profit for the system as a whole.

All of these materials and activities are paid for with money. In the same way, the resulting materials and the renewed labor force have money values, making all goods inter-convertible as elements of a continuous process in which the productive activities of various kinds of workers, sold for wages, lead by the sale of their products to the generation of sums of money to be used to reconstitute the process, to support the employers whose investment initiates the process, and to expand it through the purchase of additional workers and materials. That is, the money prices of goods and labor capacity, the form in which the elements of this production system are available for decision-making, determine the quantities of inputs and outputs of the system compatible with the investors' need to earn a profit; reciprocally, the need to minimize costs to maximize profits constrains the prices of all the elements. Given the heterogeneity of types of labor, one can construct no formula converting actual production times into money prices; instead, the mutual adjustment of prices with which sellers and buyers strive to maximize their economic advantage (in money terms) provides the only representation available of the relations among producers and between producers and consumers that constitute society as an economic system.[24]

Because money embodies the social character of the productive activity managed by the independent enterprises that make up the capitalist economy, it serves to integrate non-produced elements of the system, like land and other natural resources. Thus part of the price of gasoline is earmarked for the owners of the land where the petroleum from which it is manufactured is found, just as in the beginnings of capitalism the landed aristocracy was able to siphon off a part of the money commercial farmers made from selling the product of the agricultural workers they employed. Although money has no price, it must be paid for: interest is paid for the use of someone else's money as rent is paid for the use of someone else's land. This provides a way to assign prices to items without inherent value, like the bonds sold by businesses (and governments) to raise capital, which are worth, roughly, the amount of money that would generate the return on the bond if loaned at the going rate of interest. The prices of such items, set by supply and demand, can fluctuate wildly in response to general economic conditions.

In their independence as decision-makers from each other, entrepreneurs are potential competitors. In setting the prices they pay and charge each other they strive to shift the surplus over reproduction costs from other enterprises to their own. If a petroleum refiner can jack up the price of gasoline because other kinds of business cannot function without it, more of the profit those others might have made can flow instead to the oil company. Companies also compete by heightening productivity in their labor processes, both by making people work harder or longer for the same wage or by replacing workers with machinery that lowers costs in the long run. This, in fact, is one of the most significant long-term features of capitalism as a system, which has led to an enormous expansion of productive capacity with a diminution of the labor force relative to the quantity of product. Since this is generally accomplished by substituting machinery for laborers, it means a diminution of the investment in labor compared to that invested in raw materials, machinery, and facilities of various sorts. An unintended but useful effect of this general effort is that increasing productivity in industries producing consumption goods can allow workers to enjoy—at least for a while—a constant or improving real living standard even if wages decline as a proportion of social income (allowing more of the social working day to be spent producing to the account of employers).

As capitalism developed through the nineteenth century, each individual enterprise typically sought to cheapen its product in this way to attract a larger share of social spending. Since this goal motivates businesspeople in all areas of the economy, we would expect a general tendency to lower prices over time—that is, towards deflation—so long as the types of product do not change significantly. Against this long-term tendency must be set the effects of the changing balance of supply and demand, affected strongly across the spectrum of products by the business cycle. And in fact the typical pattern of price movements in the first century and a half of industrial capitalism was one of rising prices as business expanded in prosperity, followed by price declines when expansion turned to contraction, with average prices over the cycle tending downwards. The big exceptions were such moments as wars, when governments' attempts to pay their bills without drawing on increased production could produce bursts of inflation.

Data

Much discussion of inflation and deflation went on since capitalism got underway without real, systematic knowledge of price movements on the national and international levels. This, as we have seen, hardly prevented confident statements about the economics of money and price. The nineteenth century saw the beginning of such knowledge, with the construction of data series for prices of different kinds of goods by interested individuals who scoured a wide variety of sources. Apart from the problem of creating historical data from information that was not produced with this kind of question in mind, such as records of grain prices or wages in different areas of a country, there are also the conceptual problems raised by an economic system characterized by ongoing change in qualitative as well as quantitative terms. Unlike earlier forms of society, capitalism has involved the continual generation of new kinds of products, and constant alterations of existing kinds. It seems unproblematic to compare the price of cotton thread spun by hand with that of thread produced by a mechanized spinning jenny, but how do we conceptualize the price changes in clothing brought by the substitution of synthetic acrylic fibers for natural ones like cotton? The cost of tomatoes may be lowered by the development of fruit that can be easily shipped unripe, but given the change in taste, are we actually talking about a price change in the same food or about the substitution of a cheaper item for a different, more expensive one? Such problems emerged as practical issues when governments began to create information tracking inflation and deflation.

Much public consideration of inflation and deflation today refers to a Consumer Price Index (CPI), which tracks changes in the prices of a group of goods and services purchased by a set of consumers. Other measures of inflation measure changes in GDP for individual countries (so-called gross domestic product deflators) and even a world average; individual nations also construct measures of changes in producer prices, which follow the prices of goods at every stage of production in which they are sold for further processing or consumption. Since there is no absolute standard of price, the changes are measured relative to the prices at some moment taken as a base; as if in recognition of the lack of foundation for the concept of price in contemporary economics, these are called "real" prices, in contrast to the "nominal" prices compared to them. All of these indices require decisions to be made about which goods to consider and when goods count as the same, as well as what weights to give different categories of good in the attempt to create a numerical picture of the economy as a whole. The specification of price itself is far from straightforward, as in this small example from the field of producer prices:

> Even when several firms charge the same (or differ-ent) prices for identical commodities the true price (or price-differences) may not be revealed because of side-payments, kickbacks, etc., which are frequent occurrences. To this must be added that discriminatory treatment occurs most easily when firms are producing a great variety of commodities (e.g. steel, of which there are reportedly more than 10,000 different kinds, most having somewhat different prices from each other), and when there are great variations in the quantities bought per customer. Thus, large automobile producers will obtain a very different price of "steel" (with different ranges and frequency of fluctuations) than regional, small builders buying their "steel." A measure of "the" price of steel is, therefore, difficult to construct.

Furthermore, because "most of the individual prices which go to make up the gross national product deflator are taken from sources which include components of the Consumer Price Index and Wholesale Price Index, it is subject to the same qualifications regarding differences in quality, frequency of appearance of new products, etc."[25]

Apart from these general issues, inflation indices reflect broader economic and political currents. An interesting example is furnished by the history of the CPI in the United States. The first attempt to create such an index came between 1888 and 1890 when the newly created federal Bureau of Labor undertook a study of family expenditures and retail prices. The goal was not an academic understanding of the workings of the economy: the brief of the Bureau, a product of the Progressive era's attempt to manage rapidly developing American capitalism, was to "collect information upon the subject of labor, its relation to capital, the hours of labor, and the earnings of laboring men and women and the means of promoting their material, social, intellectual, and moral prosperity."[26] For example, Bureau data was called upon by the Anthracite Coal Commission to adjudicate a miners' strike in 1903, its data in this case justifying the award of a wage increase.

The First World War brought a call for a cost of living index to serve as the basis for wartime wage policy aimed at preserving living standards; the 12,000 families whose consumption was studied by what was now called the Bureau of Labor Statistics were defined by their working-class incomes. Similarly, during the depression of the 1930s, the Bureau's research was intended to play a role in "the promotion of labor's interests."[27] During the Second World War, however, with the new industrial unions pressing for post-depression wage increases under conditions of wartime government spending, the CPI was called on to set a cap to wages. Throughout this period—indeed, until the 1960s—the CPI measured not the change in consumer goods' prices generally but "price changes for goods customarily purchased by families of wage earners and lower-salaried workers living in large cities."[28] (For much of its history, in addition, the CPI's researches excluded single wage-earners and non-whites, just as Black workers were generally not covered by New Deal programs.) This group remained the focus of the survey after the war as CPI data became the basis for union wage agreements negotiated, in particular, in the automobile industry. In the course of the 1960s, as government transfer payments for old-age pensions, healthcare, disability, veterans' programs, and family welfare expanded, such payments were indexed to the CPI. The population studied was expanded from 45 percent to 80 percent of Americans.

As economic growth slowed and inflation accelerated, not only legislators but many economists began to argue that the CPI overstated the rate of inflation, in this way needlessly elevating government expenses as well as wage settlements. In 1978, the CPI was completely revamped in line with new theoretical prescriptions, and the official rate of inflation successfully lowered. The central change was a switch from tracking the prices of a constant group of commodities to tracking "utility" as consumer preferences changed in reaction to price changes. If beef became so expensive that buyers switched to pork, beef was replaced by pork in the prices collected by the BLS, on the theory that this preserved consumer "satisfaction," which thus defined a constant "real" standard of living. The invention of "hedonic pricing," in which different aspects of a good are accorded their own imaginary prices, allowed a good's cost to be reshaped for statistical purposes as its attributes change, for instance counting statistically as cheaper if some dimension of quality goes up while the actual price remains the same. In another curious change, while housing costs were earlier represented by data on rents, these were replaced by the cost of owned houses (including among other things mortgage payments along with house prices). Later, as house prices increased astronomically, housing costs were recomputed as the rents that homeowners would have to pay if they did not own their homes. As two experts explained, "using a rent index to represent the cost of using the services of a house might provide a better measure of changes in the cost of living to the average consumer, particularly in periods of sharp changes in costs of homes and home financing."[29]

All of this is to say that concepts underlying the various statistical series called upon to measure inflation and deflation have not only undergone serious modifications over time, limiting the meaningfulness of lengthy series, but must be taken to be highly approximate at best, and quite misleading for the most part. As Oskar Morgenstern notes, it is hard to imagine that numbers "ground out after so many steps, operations, computations, etc., all based on a great deal of theory, should *not* be correct and free from error . . . But the idea that as complex a phenomenon as the change in 'price level,' itself a heroic theoretical abstraction, could at present be measured to such a degree of accuracy [as is represented by the tenths-of-a-percentage given by official sources and newspapers] is nevertheless absurd."[30] We are well advised accordingly to pay less attention to the particular numbers furnished by official indices than to the large trends observable through the statistical fog, and often enough sensed directly by those—businesspeople and working people—who must make their way through the changing economy.

Nonetheless, in so far as such series can be constructed, we find the expected downward tendency of prices over the first half of capitalism's history, most markedly in the great period of capitalist industrialization after the mid-nineteenth century, when the mechanization of agriculture and industry spread around the world. In Schumpeter's summary, "until almost the end of the [nineteenth] century expansion in physical output was accompanied by falling prices, widespread unemployment of labor, and business losses," as firms unable to compete went out of business.[31] We find essentially the same picture with respect to prices in the numbers offered by the Minneapolis branch of the Federal Reserve System, whose economists have constructed a series depicting the cost of living in the United States from 1800 to 2022. According to their estimates, the average cost of living decreased fairly steadily until the 1920s, with the exception of three wartime periods, those around the War of 1812, the Civil War, and the First World War; the intervening periods show a steady decline in the prices of consumer goods.[32] The period since the Second World War, however, presents the unmistakable change that we have already noted: a constant inflationary tendency with occasional large surges. Statisticians at the Bank of England offer a similar account for their country, noting that "prices have risen more quickly in the last 50 years than in any similar period since 1694; the index of prices tripled between 1694 and 1948, but has risen almost 20-fold since."[33] The productivity of labor continued to increase after the war, so a general decline in prices was to be expected. Instead, prices on average rose, sometimes sharply. Clearly, something fundamental changed in world capitalism after the Second World War. If it was not simply a side effect of the end of the gold standard and even the laying of its ghost—the Bretton Woods system—what explains the inflationary tendency of postwar times?

5

Prices and Profits

We have already noted one important aspect of the story, though it may seem far from the mechanics of the price level: a new unwillingness of the groups dominating society to risk the social and political stresses brought by unemployment and impoverishment. In the nineteenth century social unrest, when it was not dissipated by emigration (often to the Americas), seemed adequately manageable by violence—by the punishment (commonly by hanging) of individual proletarians driven by abject poverty to violate the laws of private property; by the forced migration of troublesome groups (to Australia, Siberia, or other territories); and by the military suppression of wider movements. Expressions of popular discontent like that produced in England at the end of the Napoleonic wars, whose bloody denouement is known as Peterloo, and the Silesian Weavers' Revolt of 1844 were put down by armed force, as were the Paris uprisings that climaxed in the seizure of government by the Commune in 1871. This last explosion inspired fear in ruling classes everywhere; in the United States, for instance, afraid that the massive railway workers' strike of 1877 heralded communist class struggle, city fathers across the country built armories to house newly formed national guards to prepare for class war. The same impulse operated internationally: the Russian Revolution of 1917 was opposed by European and American military forces as well as White Russian armies. Likewise, what appeared to be extensions of the Russian events to Europe in 1919 were put down with bullets by governments ranging from Social Democrats in Germany to proto-fascists in Hungary.

Violence hardly vanished from the political repertory by the time of the Great Depression. Despite the decisive victory over the German revolutionary left achieved by 1923, ten years later Hitler promised the industrialists who backed him that he would eliminate any potential threat to social order from socialist and communist parties and unions—and did so with a vengeance. In the United States, the 20,000 impoverished war veterans demonstrating in Washington, DC, in 1932 for early payment of the bonus promised them were met with truncheons and machine guns. But the scale of the unfolding economic disaster, the growing militancy of both employed and unemployed workers, and the need for social unity as a precondition for war suggested the advisability of other methods, and in all the major capitalist countries attempts were made to contain the misery with welfare payments and make-work programs. In Germany, for instance, as Robert Paxton observes, "Mindful of the 1918 revolution, the Third Reich was willing to do absolutely anything to avoid unemployment or food shortages."[1] As already mentioned, the Second World War itself functioned as a massive make-work program as well as a means to reallocate spheres of economic influence among the major powers. And, in contrast to the situation after the First World War, postwar fears of a return of depression conditions together with the advent of the Cold War—which seemed to require holding sympathy for communism in Europe at bay by means of social welfare measures and meeting potential geopolitical threats by military means—kept government expenditure elevated. With respect to monetary policy, as Barry Eichengreen argues, the "commitment to full employment and growth that was integral to the postwar social compact" ruled out the "deflationary central bank policies that had redressed payments deficits under the gold standard."[2]

A real test came in 1973–5 with the return of serious recession conditions after the thirty-year Golden Age. As discussed in Chapter Two, the response of governments everywhere demonstrated an unwillingness to allow the return of a full-scale depression, with its expectable consequences of business bankruptcies, bank failures, and widespread, potentially long-lasting unemployment. Keynesian methods, far from fine-tuning the economy, had not defeated the business cycle, but they could limit its economic and social repercussions. In doing this, they also prevented the full performance of the work accomplished by depressions throughout the earlier history of capitalism: creating the possibility for renewed prosperity. While inherent in the very idea of a "business cycle," this requires some explanation.

As we have noted, in business society (to quote W. C. Mitchell) "the useful goods produced by an enterprise are not the ends of endeavor, but the means toward earning profits." Thus the state of economic affairs "depends upon the factors which affect present or prospective profits."[3] This is obvious to anyone who thinks for a moment about modern society, despite its conflict with economic dogma.[4] (Keynes, while repeating the dogma, also saw investment, and so economic growth, as responding to the "marginal productivity of capital.") This suggests that while economic downturns are produced by declines in the profitability of capital, the ensuing recession must in some way create conditions for a revival of profit-making. Clearly, for such speculations to lead anywhere, we must have some idea of the factors that determine profitability.

The classical economists, believing in an inevitable increase in wages due to the decreasing productivity of agriculture as cultivation was extended to less fertile soils, foresaw a resulting drop in profitability and consequently investment until society settled into a "stationary state." Keynes, who attempted to bring back the classical focus on questions of the production and distribution of national income, predicted something similar by generalizing the prospective decline in yield to capital investment. Neither approach, in addition to their other difficulties, accounts for the cyclical character of business fluctuations. On the other hand, non-Keynesian neoclassical general-equilibrium theory, despite its mathematical sophistication, provides "no good theory of capital or interest [which takes the place of profit in neoclassical theory] or of their relations to equilibrium prices," as even a sympathetic student of economic methodology recognizes. Economists "do not understand why the rate of interest is generally positive (and thus how it is that capitalism can work) ... how large-scale technological changes will affect wages and interest or how changes in the rate of profits will affect innovation."[5] It is not surprising, therefore, that this tradition has produced little in the way of a satisfactory theory of the business cycle.[6]

Contemporary approaches to business-cycle theory rely for the most part on the idea of "shocks," accidentally produced by ill-conceived monetary policy or events like a war or a pandemic, that knock the economy out of equilibrium. As a result, each economic fluctuation tends to receive a particular explanation, rather than a general one that would explain this recurrent phenomenon.[7] Mitchell, who eschewed formal theorizing in his lifelong investigation of business cycles, laid the blame for "the recurrent disorders which constitute crises and depressions" on "the bewildering complexity of the task" faced by businessmen in "guiding economic activity."[8] This approach also fails to account either for the regular recurrence of such events or for what seem like structural changes in business-cycle phenomena over time. Given the general lack of a basic understanding of capitalist dynamics, the record of economists' failure in predicting and controlling economic events is hardly surprising.

The elephant in the room of economic theory is, of course, Marx's prediction of the tendency of the rate of profit to fall along with the progress of the capitalist economy, a theory with the attractive feature of accounting for the recurrent phenomena of the cycle of prosperity and depression in terms of known features of capitalism as a system. Viewing money as a representation of social productive activity, Marx argued that the increasing mechanization of that activity undertaken as part of competitive cost-cutting implied a reduction of actual labor performed relative to past labor embodied in technology and the enlarged mass of raw materials processed. Profit—the money representation of the surplus of productive activity over that required to produce the goods consumed by workers and used in the production process—could therefore be expected to decline relative to total investment. That is, the increased productivity of labor responsible for price decreases, due to increased efficiency in organization and mechanization, would at the same time mean a general decline in profitability.[9]

Marx's hypothesis concerns the surplus labor time, embodied in goods exchanged for money, performed in the world economy taken as a whole; the object of competitive struggle among economic entities, this money takes the forms of interest, rents, and taxes as well as of what Marx called "profit of industry," the returns claimed by individual businesses. Nevertheless, its quantitative changes set limits to the profits seizable by capitalist enterprises. Its decline will eventually show up in a slowdown of investment, bringing a diminishing demand for workers, and therefore for their consumption goods, and for investment goods. As sales begin to contract instead of expand, people can't pay their bills; credit tightens, producing the financial difficulties characteristic of business downturns, such as stock-market collapses and bank failures. Growing unemployment and business failures lead to further declining demand and falling prices. On the other hand, as both production goods and labor become cheaper, with the productivity of labor unchanged or, typically, even improved, the profitability of surviving business enterprises rises, producing a new upswing, eventually earning a new extension of credit facilities. In this way the depression itself creates the basis for a new prosperity. From this point of view, it was the worldwide downturn lasting from the 1920s to the end of the Second World War that prepared the way for the postwar Golden Age. Marx's argument is a highly abstract one, but the return of profitability problems in the mid-1970s certainly gave it greater plausibility than the Keynesian claim to have tamed the business cycle, not to mention the orthodox neoclassical idea of a self-equilibrating system.

If the basic problem Marx diagnosed applies throughout capitalism's history, it is also true that the system's evolution introduces new elements. For instance, the rising productivity of labor in the postwar expansion, building on the industrialization of the nineteenth century, meant not only that less labor was required to produce a growing quantity of goods, but that more labor had to be engaged in selling those goods, including, for example, the expansion of various modes of advertising. The activity of selling—of seeing to it that goods are exchanged for money—is an expense for the production system as a whole, paid out of the surplus created in production and therefore further lowering the profitability on investment. While efforts are made—notably by means of computerization—to limit the amount of labor required for such purposes, they are harder to automate than production processes. The same is true for the growing labor forces required by the expansion of state-financed social services like education and healthcare.[10]

Whatever its explanation, capitalism's old problem of recurrent recession reappeared in the 1970s. But at this time, especially under the new circumstances of the apparent threat of communism, those who managed the capitalist economies were not prepared for a rerun of the process by which depression prepared the ground for a new prosperity. The alternative, as we have seen, was the expansion of the mixed economy, in which government spending, on welfare measures or on the production of infrastructure or military materiel, kept the socially disruptive symptoms of capitalism's recessionary tendencies at bay. As already noted, this requires governments to tax or borrow the money required for such operations, with taxation reducing the amount of profit available for profit-seeking investment and borrowing putting off repayment (and interest) to future taxation or further borrowing.

From the Keynesian point of view, government spending is just an expansion of demand, or an additional investment in future production. After all, if the goal of production is consumption, what does it matter if the good produced is a $4 million cruise missile paid for by the Defense Department, rather than a computer destined for a factory production line? A concept like GDP, and that of the growth of GDP, similarly ignore the difference between profit-seeking and non-profit spending. Once we remember that the goal of capitalist production is the earning of a return on investment, however, things look different. The producer of the computer sells its machine for more than it paid to make it; this is possible because the computer's price, representing the activity of making it, exceeds the costs of the labor and materials employed. Similarly, the business that uses the computer to produce a truck, because it invests its own capital in the process, gets to keep whatever profit production and sale of the truck make possible. But the profit made by the defense contractor when it sells the missile to the armed forces was originally taken (or borrowed) by the government from the private sector as a whole. It is merely redistributed to those companies favored with government contracts. And the government makes no money by using the missile, however useful it may be to obliterate a building in another country. Capital is not produced but consumed by governments; state spending does not solve the problem of insufficient profitability. It is an expense for the capitalist economy.[11]

This is why, whatever theories of the economy they may hold, businesspeople generally hate taxes and worry when government borrowing leads to large deficits and the future tax increases they promise. However obscurely they understand it, government spending represents a deduction from the funds they have appropriated from the process of hiring labor and selling the products. In theory, money used to boost the economy in a recessionary moment should be paid back when growth resumes under its own steam. But over the long term the payback has not come, and the amount consumed by the state has increased steadily over the last 75 years. To take some numbers from United States history, that country's national debt was $17 billion in 1929; ten years later it had reached $40 billion. A year after the war's end, 1946, it reached a high of $269 billion. Rising through the 300s, it jumped to $620 billion by 1976 and from then on rose steadily to its 2022 value of $30,824 billion.[12] Insistence on the necessity of balanced budgets has had to give way to the insouciance shown just a few years ago about public debts equaling or exceeding GDP. Internationally, the amounts borrowed by poor countries from rich ones has similarly expanded without cease; it is clear that, for instance, Egypt, Sri Lanka, Pakistan, and Somalia are never going to be able to repay their debts. But neither will the United States.

Of course, once in place, the apparatus of public spending acquires an interest of its own and a tendency towards expansion.[13] But more than this, in the absence of sufficient self-generated growth, capitalism has become dependent for its continued existence, under conditions so far acceptable to the vast majority of its denizens, on state spending—from the provision of roads, education, and healthcare to emergency feeding programs wherever capitalism has created humanitarian disasters, to the preparation for and practice of war still basic to the competitive struggle for control of the earth's resources. The American "military-industrial complex" identified by President Eisenhower in his farewell speech to the nation has been supplemented by a health-industrial, an education-industrial, and even a prison-industrial complex.

Elsewhere throughout the world, the state and the private economy are intimately bound together in numerous ways, from government participation in energy companies to the sovereign wealth funds central to economic affairs in Norway, Singapore, and Saudi Arabia. A cessation of government spending—now responsible worldwide for at least 40 percent of economic activity as measured by GDP—would plunge the world into a depression of unimaginable depth. It was widely agreed, for instance, that a failure to expand government credits to bail out the financial system in the face of the 2008 crisis would have led to a general collapse of the world economy.[14]

The Age of Credit

We thus have a situation in which an underlying insufficiency of profitability is complemented by a constant increase in unprofitable spending by the state. This spending appears as market demand in excess of what the economy would generate on its own, at least so long as the credit (government debt) on which it is based can be rolled over and expanded. And this in turn supports a new response by capitalist firms to the insufficiency of profit: competition by price maintenance, or increases, rather than by price-cutting. This was, after all, the whole point of government intervention into the market economy: the expansion of investment in production goods and labor despite inadequate profits. As a result, deflation ceased to be the main response to declines in growth; inflation took its place. In 1971, Arthur Burns, recently appointed chair of the Federal Reserve System, noted in a meeting of the Open Market Committee that

The old rules were no longer working... Years ago, when business activity turned down, prices would respond—with some lag, not by rising more slowly but by declining; and wages would follow. That kind of response had become progressively weaker after World War I, and of late one found that at a time when unemployment was increasing prices continued to advance at an undiminished pace and wages rose at an increasing pace.[15]

This phenomenon, whose existence was hotly debated with the 2021 uptick of inflation, was widely recognized in the 1970s. According to one August 1974 article in the *New York Times*, for example, increased profitability of American corporations reflected less gains in productivity than "inventory profits," when "the price of the final product has reflected up-to-date costs of materials to a much greater extent than the actual costs of the materials." In the previous year, "so-called inventory profits accounted for nearly 60 per cent of the total increase of reported profits."[16] Another profit-booster was the accelerated depreciation of capital goods, which entered as costs in forming the prices of finished goods. But apart from accounting gimmicks and tax manipulations, the whole structure of price formation had altered, including such features as cost-of-living adjustments to social-welfare payments and labor contracts.

As W. David Slawson pointed out in 1981, "The last time that agricultural goods produced in the United States suffered massive price decreases was during the Great Depression, before government pricing institutions were established for them."[17] By 2020 government assistance provided 46 percent of net farm income, countering market pressures.[18] In many areas beyond agriculture government subsidies—local ones in the form of municipal tax abatements or national ones in the form of price supports wangled for favored companies or whole industries—support pricing increases, or price stability offsetting productivity increases. More generally, in Slawson's words, "with or without government assistance, virtually everyone enjoys the protections of a pricing institution for the prices that constitute his principal source of profits or income."[19] Though this state of affairs had been developing since the Great Depression, it was given a shove by the declining profitability manifested in the downturn of 1973–5: in Slavin's words, "competitive inflation did not really begin in earnest in the United States until late in 1973," ignited by the "quadrupling of world oil prices simultaneously with some sharp increases in food prices caused by shortages."

> When OPEC first raised oil prices, some in the United States predicted that oil sales would decline sharply and that OPEC would break apart as a result. When this did not happen but, on the contrary, not only the OPEC countries but all the international oil companies made enormous profits, price setters in other industries were quick to pick the lesson up.[20]

Naturally, in the course of this process, all prices are not raised simultaneously. The prices of items like petroleum, on which the world's economy depends, can be hoisted more easily than those of some other goods. In particular, wages rise more slowly than the prices of consumption goods, which boosts profitability for capital as a whole by redistributing income from workers to the class of employers. This tactic cannot be pursued without limit, however, as eventually workers put up resistance to it, so that over time wage increases contribute to the general increase in the price level. (From the business point of view, as we have already noted, labor costs are the root of the problem of inflation.)

Price increases, which imply a declining value of money, require increases in the supply of money that people can spend, if the level of demand is to match the higher-priced supply of goods. This requirement was met not only by the steady expansion of government debt but by the ballooning of private credit. As Duncan Foley explains it, briefly but clearly,

> Given the value of money, the monetary and credit mechanisms face the problem of financing the flow of commodity purchases and sales at that level of the value of money. In modern capitalist economies this problem is solved primarily by the expansion and contraction of credit. In the first instance, this expansion of credit is inherent in the private transactions of capitalist firms, since they depend on private credit to finance most transactions. Specific regulation of certain sectors of the credit markets, like the reserve requirements imposed in the United States on commercial banks, serve to determine the relative share of the total credit transactions that pass through those sectors, and the price the banks, for instance, can charge for their services in facilitating credit.[21]

The generally Keynesian bias of postwar thinking, in addition to supplying money by way of government spending, kept interest rates low and the money supply loose for a few decades. But, as Foley suggests, the growing independence of credit from the central bank-generated money supply marks another important change from the pre-Second World War situation. In the words of Moritz Schularick and Alan Taylor,

> Our ancestors lived in an Age of Money, where credit was closely tied to money, and formal analysis could use the latter as a proxy for the former. Today, we live in a different world, an Age of Credit, where financial innovation and regulatory ease broke that link, setting in motion an unprecedented expansion of the role of credit in the macroeconomy.[22]

What these authors mean by "money" are the coins and notes issued by state authorities (M1), as opposed to the bank-created deposits (M2) and other forms of lending they call "credit." In the Age of Money—roughly, 1870 to 1939—money and credit grew and shrank together, maintaining a stable relation to GDP; in the Age of Credit—the period since 1945—credit expanded rapidly, far out of proportion to the central bank-produced money supply, both the credit on which business runs as a matter of course and consumer credit. Credit extended to businesses makes possible their continuous functioning and expansion while goods are produced, moved to market, and sold. It can expand to accommodate increased prices of raw materials, transportation costs, and the like. Similarly, consumer credit makes possible the maintenance or improvement of living standards even without important wage growth; by the same token it facilitates rising prices of consumer goods. (The use of credit cards has regularized price creep; not only does it obscure price changes by delaying the actual moment of payment, but merchants pass on the fees they pay credit companies to their customers, who for the most part pay the higher prices even when they are using cash.) In addition to the higher prices for goods facilitated by the use of credit purchase, the latter increases costs, since the interest paid is effectively part of the price. In the case of housing, mortgage interest can double the cost of a house. That some of the money flows to a bank and not to the seller of the house does not alter the fact of a transfer of money from buyers to owners of capital. Particularly in the United States, which saw a great expansion of home ownership after the Second World War, the increasing value of homes, against which people could borrow money for further spending, supported rising prices. As Aglietta and Orléan observed in 1984, "Having become an essential element of the defense of living conditions, households' demand for credit, made possible by the modern financial system, is now a powerful factor of inflation."[23]

In addition to bank-created credit money, the turn of the twenty-first century saw an additional expansion of money (or near-money) with the development of "shadow banking." This term refers to the financial activities of so-called nonbanks— repo facilities, hedge funds, pension funds, money-market funds, mortgage operations, various kinds of investment vehicles, exchange traded funds, and so on—often highly leveraged and vastly expanding the money available to borrowers. Many of these entities were spun off from banks in order to escape the degree of regulation to which banks are still subject. Making particular use of devices like securitization, in which existing debt of various degrees of reliability is repackaged in new debt instruments yielding different rates of return depending on their riskiness, the expansion of "shadow money" contributed greatly to the financial collapse of 2008 (and is going on its merry way at the present time).[24]

The expansion of credit was a global story: Schularick and Taylor's data are drawn from fourteen major capitalist economies. It is a story not just of continuing economic expansion but of structural change, as finance became a more important economic sector relative to manufacturing and commerce. In the course of this development, the expansion of credit created "an age of unprecedented financial risk and leverage" on which an expanding economy came to depend.[25] The decline in profitability inspired a search for returns on investment outside of manufacturing, and funds available thanks to the expansion of credit were put to work chasing short-term gains in financial speculation. Hence the series of asset bubbles, with leveraged investment in stocks, real estate, commodities (notably oil and metals) and even invented assets like cryptocurrency providing quick, large gains for some followed by enormous losses for others. All of this needed to be backed up periodically by central banks, responsible, for instance, for cleaning up the mess when a third of American savings and loans institutions collapsed between 1986 and 1995 because of bad bets on real estate, at a total cost of $160 billion (with $132 billion paid out of tax revenue). The readiness of the central bank system to play the role of lender of last resort naturally strengthened the tendency toward risk-taking by creditors and debtors alike, especially since

> the increasing dependence of the banking system on access to funding from financial markets could also mean that central banks are forced to underwrite the entire funding market in times of distress in order to avoid the collapse of

the banking system, as witnessed in 2008–09. This "mission creep" follows from the fact that banking stability can no longer rest on the foundations of deposit insurance alone, with the Lender of Last Resort now having to confront wholesale (i.e., nondeposit) bank runs.[26]

Thus the collapse of Silicon Valley Bank (the USA's sixteenth largest) in early 2023 motivated the FDIC to ignore the $250,000 limit set by law and guarantee deposits *in toto*. In China, where the government effectively controls the banking system, banks were required to play the role of lender of last resort in 2022, by making available $56 billion to support a collapsing real estate sector, which in the wake of 2008 had been encouraged by way of easy credit to undertake building projects all over the country.[27] Another dimension of this phenomenon is the loans advanced to whole countries, like Mexico in 1980, to prevent a default on earlier loans that would have destroyed the American banking system that had provided many of those loans.

More recently the offsetting of inadequate profitability by credit expansion has taken the strange form of what have come to be called "zombie" firms, with low or negative profits, maintaining a simulacrum of life thanks to constant infusions of debt via the junk bond market. By 2020, zombies accounted "for 16 percent of all the publicly traded companies in the United States, and more than 10 percent in Europe, according to the Bank for International Settlements, the bank for central banks."[28] The most spectacular cases of such businesses are those which were born zombies, such as Uber and WeWork, whose revenue growth has been accompanied by capital losses in the billions and which are kept in motion only thanks to constant transfusions of credit (from such nonbank sources as the Saudi sovereign wealth fund and the SoftBank investment fund). Despite their unprofitability, rides in Uber's cars—subsidized by the continuous inflow of money (and downward pressure on drivers' wages)—have become more expensive over time.

By the end of 2019 the debt load of non-financial companies had reached an all-time high, attesting both to their failure to generate profits sufficient for their needs and to the ability of banks (and nonbanks) to create the money required to stave off systemic collapse. Global finance has increased since the 1980s to four times the value of world goods production; China's corporate debt alone grew to $20 trillion. "In the United States, against the backdrop of decades-long access to cheap money, non-financial corporations have seen their debt burdens more than double from $3.2 trillion in 2007 to $6.6 trillion in 2019."[29] Many firms turned from public ownership to private equity to avoid financial regulation; by 2020 private equity firms had debts equal to 600 percent of those firms' annual earnings. This debt represents a bet on future profits, and one that is far from sure: even from the point of view of the official rating system, biased toward the encouragement of speculative investment, 51 percent of corporate bonds issued in 2019 were classified as BBB, the lowest rating. Twenty-five percent were junk bonds, unrated because below investment grade.[30] For the present, however, all this extra money has provided an alternative to the deflationary depressions of the past, as the creation of money by bank credit and the further expansion of the money supply in the form of shadow money allowed inflation to substitute for systemic profitability despite periodic deflations of the bubbles thus created for stock, bond, real estate, and other assets from which returns are sought.[31]

6

From the Great Inflation to Magic Money

The Great Inflation of the 1970s in the United States was based on the expansion of government borrowing to pay for the Vietnam War, to which was added a vast increase of government civil spending and transfer payments in the name of the Great Society, even though the Johnson government insisted on cutting taxes in 1964. In contrast to the period of the Korean War, when inflation was somewhat checked by the imposition of price controls, during the Vietnam War "price controls were avoided—in spite of the obvious signs of a booming economy, such as attainment of the highest level of capacity utilization and lowest level of unemployment since World War II," which supported large price increases after 1965.[1] Despite the common ascription of the basis of the Great Inflation to the 1971 end of the Bretton Woods system, the expansion of the money supply this supposedly made possible, and the first oil shock, the "inflation of the 1970s and early 1980s was initiated by events that preceded by at least a half-decade President Nixon's termination in August 1971 of the convertibility of dollars into gold, and OPEC's raising of oil prices in 1973–74 in response to the Yom Kippur War and the erosion of its real dollar income."[2] Far from being a "monetary phenomenon" provoked by excessive government deficits, examination of the advanced capitalist nations as a group reveals, "the extent to which a nation experienced inflation or stability in prices, relative to other nations, depended very much on its performance, relative to other nations, in the world economy over an extended period." Thus nations with current-account surpluses, like Japan and Germany, saw relatively small price increases at the time.[3]

However sincere his belief in Milton Friedman's theories may have been, Fed chairman Paul Volcker must have understood that his attempts to constrict the money supply would raise interest rates and thereby restrict the flow of credit across the economy, producing downward pressure on employment and limiting wage increases, always identified as a major cause of inflation. As we saw, the effects of Volcker's policy were in fact devastating, and not just for the national economy. Indeed it is true that if it becomes more expensive to borrow money businesses and households will borrow less of it, with immediate effects on the sales and so the prices of producer goods and the wages that pay for consumer goods. As credit becomes harder to get, so that, for example, rising mortgage costs crimp the housing industry and car loans become more expensive, average prices will stop rising or fall.

Volcker's success in producing this result was aided by the fact that the world economy entered into a recession in 1980, lasting until 1983, with high business failure and unemployment rates across the globe, suggesting that some other processes were underway besides those due to the belief in Monetarism in the United States and Great Britain. This was underlined by the failure of the monetary reforms to produce renewed prosperity. As William Greider reminds us,

Starting in 1979, Volcker had regularly predicted that curbing inflation would revive long-term investment in the American economy. The improved climate for capital formation, he said, would lead to greater growth in productivity, the key to larger income shares for everyone in the future. Abroad, the restored value of the dollar would bring stability to the international financial system.

In fact... expansion of economic output in the eighties was roughly one-third less than real economic growth during the previous decade. Real disposable incomes grew more slowly and so did the creation of new jobs. Productivity gains, already weak and troubling in the seventies, were slightly worse in the eighties. Unemployment was persistently higher than ever before.[4]

By raising interest rates Volcker had exposed the internal weakness of the capitalist economy at this time; the economic system, not generating sufficient profit, was dependent for at least some of its growth on government spending and low-cost credit. Inflation had taken the place of recession; the policies that moderated inflation allowed the recession to manifest itself more fully.

The Monetarist experiment therefore led not to the abandonment or even the diminution of state economic activity but to its redirection. Despite Ronald Reagan's insistence on the evil character of government spending, the continued weakness of the capitalist economy did not permit an actual end to it—in fact, the national debt rose to then record levels under his presidency. But the modality of government economic intervention evolved away from the maintenance of "maximum employment" and the limitation of social suffering towards the subsidization of select corporations, either directly or by the device of privatization, transferring such governmental functions as education, imprisonment, and even war-making to private businesses. Governments around the world reacted to the continuing decline of capitalist prosperity by cutting state payments for health, welfare, pensions, education, and unemployment relief—even U.S. military spending fell significantly from the mid-1980s to the turn of the century— while tax cuts and government subsidization programs shifted wealth increasingly towards a small group of businesspeople. The Eurozone set statutory limits to budget deficits and national debt levels for member states, on the theory that strict control of fiscal activity would protect the value of the euro and maintain the economic strength of the bloc of countries using it.

The highpoint of privatization came with the collapse of the Soviet Union in 1989 and Russia's full engagement with the global capitalist economy, soon followed by China's rapid integration into world markets. These developments were accompanied by a relaxation of international trade and capital restrictions that saw international bank loans grow from 27 percent to 56 percent of global GDP between 1990 and 2007. "Neoliberalism" and "globalization" worked together to create something hailed as a new world economic order, based increasingly on flows of finance.

Seeking to increase profitability, companies moved production to relatively low-wage areas of Asia, Central America, and Eastern Europe. This, together with the economic expansion of China, Russia, India, and other "emerging economies," lowered production costs, contributing to keeping inflation levels low after the 1980s. "The core mechanism," as economist Kenneth Rogoff explained in a talk sponsored by the Federal Reserve Bank of Kansas City in 2006, comes through greater competition that weakens the power of domestic monopolies and labor unions. Greater competition contributes to greater price and wage flexibility, and diminishes the output gains to be reaped from expansionary monetary policy for any given inflation impulse.[5]

Rogoff noted, however, that while the "Great Moderation" of economic indicators aided by globalization included the "sharp decline in the volatility of real output" that one would expect to go along with price stability, it also brought high "volatility of asset prices," including equities, housing, and foreign exchange.[6] This was, it would turn out, prescient. On the one hand, it was the collapse in the American housing bubble a year after Rogoff's talk that sparked the Great Recession of 2008, requiring massive intervention by the world's economic authorities. On the other, that intervention did not lead to the expected increase in consumer-price inflation.

Japan had already experienced a version of the worldwide downturn to come when a giant real-estate bubble in that country burst at the end of the 1980s. The underlying cause of Japan's difficulties may be traced, paradoxically, to its success as an industrial export powerhouse. In order to keep the yen undervalued, supporting exports, the dollars (and other currencies) earned from exports were not exchanged for yen usable for investment in Japan but recycled into the American and other foreign economies. Though there was little growth in productive capacity, the Japanese financial authorities "were successful during the 1980s in fostering an expansion in bank credit that far outstripped the expansion of the real economy," facilitating "two of the greatest asset bubbles in history," in equities and real estate.[7] When they collapsed, the authorities could do little to counteract the downturn by pushing already low interest rates below zero. Instead, the Bank of Japan tried out a program of asset purchases under the name of Quantitative Easing or QE (量的緩和, *ryoteki kanwa*): buying government bonds and asset-backed securities and equities, the Bank pumped ¥30 trillion ($300 billion) into the commercial banking system over four years. QE had little effect on the low-profit, low-investment domestic economy, especially as companies preferred to use their money to deleverage rather than to expand further. Government spending on public works, social security, local tax grants, and debt service, increasing continuously after 1991, maintained GDP growth, but state debt rose from 40 percent of GDP in 1991 to nearly 220 percent by 2022.[8] Despite massive monetary loosening and fiscal stimulus, not only consumer prices and wages but asset prices remained low, and the low-growth economy actually entered deflationary territory (providing one more disproof of Keynesianism and Monetarism alike).

After 2008, particularly in the United States, QE helped avoid recession and deflation in the wake of the financial crisis. Unlike classical deficit spending, the money used for QE was not acquired by taxation—since this would defeat the purpose of supporting business—or borrowing from private owners of wealth. Instead central banks—in the case of the USA, the Federal Reserve—followed the Japanese example, expanding their liabilities ("printing money," if only electronically) to buy Treasuries and private debt, such as mortgage-backed bonds, from private financial institutions.[9] This injected money into the financial system, in the form of increased interest-earning reserves held by banks. That the money for the most part stayed in those banks suggests limited demand for funds for productive investment; as in earlier decades, low profitability made investment in industry unattractive. Low interest rates by keeping bond yields low both raised bond prices and pushed investors towards the stock market, creating an international bull market in equities. Basically, none of this cost business anything, while the rise in securities prices particularly benefited the super-wealthy minority who disproportionately own stocks and bonds. It had little effect on wages, which continued to stagnate or decline.

In fact, the same decade in the United States witnessed what political-economy journalist Annie Lowrey called an "affordability crisis," as "families were bled dry by landlords, hospital administrators, university bursars, and child-care centers." (Similar tales could be told of other "advanced economies" at this time.) Writing in 2020, before the official advent of renewed inflation, she noted that

> Viewing the economy through a cost-of-living paradigm helps explain why roughly two in five American adults would struggle to come up with $400 in an emergency so many years after the Great Recession ended. It helps explain why one in five adults is unable to pay the current month's bills in full. It demonstrates why a surprise furnace-repair bill, parking ticket, court fee, or medical expense remains ruinous for so many American families, despite all the wealth this country has generated. Fully one in three households is classified as "financially fragile."[10]

Soaring prices in these areas limited the possibility of raising prices on everyday consumer goods. Inflation as measured by the CPI and similar indices remained relatively low, even while speculative asset prices—real-estate, stocks, art, and even the old mainstay, gold—rose spectacularly (the S&P index of equity prices, for instance, rose 650 percent between 2009 and 2020).

With their focus on consumer prices, experts wondered during the decade after 2010, "Why is inflation so low?" After all, expanding the money supply was supposed to have deleterious consequences for the price system. Economists working for the Federal Reserve System pointed out that the missing inflation was "a concern around the world," because "very low inflation is typically associated with an increased probability of falling into deflation . . . a phenomenon associated with weak economic conditions." Exploring a range of explanations for the failure of inflation to appear, they came up with the idea that "the new sharing economy"—they give the example of Airbnb accommodations for travellers—"and the demographic transition" to an older workforce are "the most likely explanations."[11] On the other hand, economists pondering "the inflation puzzle in the euro area" at the Centre for Economic Policy Research in 2019 found that "inflation decline is mostly to be attributed to . . . long-term expectations."[12] Two years later those expectations, if they existed, were proved wrong. Neither the "sharing economy" nor the aging of the population had disappeared when inflation came roaring back in 2021.

One reason for low inflation measures in the second decade of the twenty-first century was that a recession was well on the way before the COVID-19 pandemic tipped the world economy over the edge. During the last quarter of 2019 Japan's GDP slumped by 6.3 percent to a growth rate of −1.6 percent, while Germany's GDP growth (and this is the world's fourth-largest economy) fell to zero.

Europe as a whole claimed 1.1 percent growth in 2019. Among the economically stronger countries, China's growth rate of 6 percent was the lowest it had been in thirty years, and u.s. gdp, with flat growth in the last quarter, increased by only 2.3 percent in 2019, the lowest increase since 2016.[13]

When the pandemic hit, national governments, unprepared for the medical emergency despite decades of warnings, reacted after deadly delays by limiting social movement to control the infection rate, effectively putting the economy into an induced recessionary coma. A cascade of business closures produced mass worklessness on a scale rivaling that of the Great Depression. The evaporation of stock and bond values that came with the collapse of economic activity wiped out pensions and nest eggs, along with some percentage of hedge funds. The Federal Reserve took swift action to support equity prices, while governments around the world pumped trillions of dollars (and other currencies) into transfer payments and other forms of economic stimulus (most of it, naturally, flowing directly to businesses). Even in the midst of what amounted to a serious economic crisis, some policy experts expressed anxiety that expanded government spending would produce uncontrolled inflation. But others pointed to the experience of the post-2008 bailouts to pooh-pooh the danger; now used to low inflation, these economists and politicians breezily waved away worries about government deficits. If anything, deflation was the danger. After all, the alternative was clearly a global economic catastrophe. Still, the ever-growing deficit was successfully invoked by politicians in the United States who opposed the multitrillion-dollar "Build Back Better" bill proposed by the Biden administration, though funds continued to flow into the financial system.

After a year of COVID shutdown, the business class seemed to have decided that enough was enough. Pandemic or no pandemic, whatever the toll of illness and death, it was time for people to go back to work, and for business to make money again. In the USA, expanded unemployment payments and monthly stipends for children came to an end, along with modest "hero pay" for "essential workers." Elsewhere, too, special programs to support economic life were phased out. Workers began to be rehired as businesses reopened; in the meantime many people had been able to increase their savings due to the combination of stimulus payments and business closures, which limited spending opportunities. One result was a surge of spending at a moment of relatively limited and dislocated supply, offering an opportunity for companies to make up for the lost year. In particular, increases in energy prices (which had dropped radically during the shutdown), wholesale costs, and shipping costs were passed along to consumers, producing a marked increase in inflation gauges.

The Federal Reserve stopped downplaying the significance of rising prices after the Employment Cost Index released on October 29, 2021 showed that wages and benefits were rising faster than expected (mostly at the lower end of the scale). Even though wages were, as usual, lagging behind prices, this was enough to revive worries about the wage–price spiral that is supposed to have enabled the inflation of the 1970s. Accordingly, "Executives spent last quarter warning about higher wages and shipping costs." Luckily, "In the end, many companies were able to raise their prices by as much as, or more than, the increase in costs . . . So even with the highest inflation in decades [*sic*], reported profit margins are expected to be high—and rising."[14]

One of the odd features of the discussion of inflation, both in news media and among economists, is its hypostatization as an autonomous force. The Federal Reserve, we are told, is attempting to "wrestle inflation under control"; inflationary forces "drive up prices." In reality, as we have seen, inflation is an outcome of economic decision-making: specifically decisions to increase prices, at the present time often involving decisions to limit supply as a way of forestalling competitive price-cutting. An inflationary process is a struggle for control over social resources, as Michel Aglietta and André Orléan suggested by linking money and violence in the title of their book on monetary questions.[15] For instance, they point out that the German hyperinflation of the early 1920s resulted from

> the success of the ruling classes ... in escaping any appropriation of their wealth [to pay the government's debts]. They obtained this result by way of a massive export of capital but also by their attitude, negligent to say the least, towards inflation.

Such factors also explain how the inflation could be brought to an end "from one day to the next" by the monetary reform that introduced the rentenmark: as the Social Democratic Party lost control of government, "a consensus was created among the [dominant] social layers to put an end to the speculative conditions of money creation."[16]

It is true that businesses are making pricing decisions today in response to a state of affairs—the decline of profitability— certainly unintended by them. And there is the background idea, by now baked into policy thinking, of avoiding another Great Depression. But, given these conditions, raising prices is a competitive tactic, chosen among possible alternatives. Despite the bewilderment of economists, the springs of price increases on this occasion were not so hard to see. What is less easy to understand is the relation between the causes of rising prices—even on the official account—and the remedy universally agreed upon, the raising of interest rates by central banks.

Paul Volcker's Ghost

The official story circa 2022 was that inflation, caused by an imbalance between government-stimulated demand and supply limited by supply-chain shocks and the war in Ukraine, was damaging the economy and in particular squeezing wage-earners, who are regularly evoked as the object of central bankers' tender regard. (This may have reached its apogee in a 2021 *Washington Post* story about the Fed chairman's concern for the homeless of Washington, DC: "The people living in those tents had no idea that their burgeoning village kept this man, Federal Reserve Chair Jerome H. Powell, up at night, or that he kept thinking about them as he drove two blocks south to his office."[17]) And so the Fed, and other central banks, must counteract inflation by slowing economic expansion, weakening sales, upping the number of business failures, and provoking increased unemployment (and no doubt homelessness). Because people—both workers and businesspeople—will then have less money, society-wide demand for goods will shrink; with demand more closely aligned with supply, prices will fall. The obvious contradiction is usually resolved with the idea that a short burst of present pain for the working class will produce a stable economy with more and better-paid jobs in the future.

This was not a new story: Jerome Powell named his inspiration when he called Paul Volcker "the greatest economic public servant of [his] era."[18] Just as fifty years ago inflation was blamed on union power and government spending, today businesspeople and economists discover the threat of future runaway inflation in the faint stirrings of worker self-defense, which have yet to make much headway against a half-century's relentless attack on wages. "It's a risk that we simply can't run," Powell, who has called the labor market "unsustainably hot," said at a news conference in May 2022. "We can't allow a wage–price spiral to happen."[19]

Why can't the problem be solved by increasing supply rather than decreasing demand? For one thing, it's not free: to increase the supply of oil, for instance, wells would have to be drilled, refineries reopened, and workers hired. All this would cost money, which would have to be justified by enlarged future returns. Thus, according to a *New York Times* article of April 27, 2022, "The biggest reason oil production is not increasing is that U.S. energy companies and Wall Street investors are not sure that prices will stay high long enough for them to make a profit from drilling lots of new wells." The Saudis are not interested in increasing the petroleum supply either, no doubt for the same reason. As a result, production fell so low that a considerable number of American refineries were closed. The Texas company ExxonMobil announced in December 2022 that its focus was "on funneling the proceeds from elevated prices back to investors, rather than spending profits on new drilling."[20]

A similar story holds for other goods whose control by a small number of corporations makes price-setting easy, such as meat, eggs, restaurant meals, and many other items whose increasing cost is bedeviling consumers. "Although food companies are prominent examples of how rapid inflation is being passed from producers to consumers," the *New York Times* noted in November 2022,

> the trend is evident across a wide variety of industries. Executives from banks, airlines, hotels, consumer goods companies and other firms have said they are finding that customers have money to spend and can tolerate higher prices.[21]

Rising rents are commonly blamed on the limited housing stock, but more to the point is the international buying-up of swaths of housing by venture-capitalist firms aiming at quick profits from jacked-up rents. That is no doubt a better use for the money than building low-income housing. In general, if they could make more money by expanding production, companies would already be doing it, not stashing their cash in offshore banks and nonbanks, distributing it as dividends to investors, or investing it in speculative ventures like buying up the world's houses. Meanwhile, companies, whose cash flow suffered during the COVID-19 recession, are making money the way things are. Everybody wants to end inflation but nobody wants to cut their profits by producing more and charging less.

When probed, the official explanation of why demand must be cut rather than supply expanded rests on economic theorizing at quite a distance from events reported in newspapers. Trying to figure out the coexistence of unemployment and inflation in the 1970s, some economists came up with the idea of the Non-Accelerating Inflation Rate of Unemployment (or NAIRU), the level of joblessness at which inflation does not increase.[22] This notion, a descendant of Milton Friedman's conception of a "natural rate of unemployment" (although its inventors sharply rejected Friedman's claim that inflation was primarily a monetary phenomenon[23]), now guides the Fed in its making of monetary policy. The postwar goal of full employment has long been discarded. A product of neoclassical theory, the NAIRU cannot be directly observed but only inferred—if the theory is correct—from the movement of wages and prices as unemployment rises. In 2019 Federal Reserve chairman Powell acknowledged that, "Since 2012, declining unemployment has had surprisingly little effect on inflation, prompting a steady decline in estimates of" the natural rate.[24] Nonetheless, he testified at a congressional hearing, "we need the concept of a natural rate of unemployment" to "have some sense of whether unemployment is high, low, or just right."[25] In fact, there is no evidence that such a number as the NAIRU exists; since the relation between inflation and unemployment is thought even by its proponents to vary over time, there is no direct empirical test of the theory. Nonetheless, the idea of the NAIRU lies behind the wish that the Fed, while fighting inflation, can achieve a "soft landing"—that is, raise interest rates to just the point that stops inflation without provoking a "serious" recession, leaving unemployment "just right."

One of the most fascinating (and influential) discussions of the inflation issue, published in 2022, however, makes no use of the "natural rate" idea. In fact, economic theory plays hardly any role in the *Annual Economic Report* for 2022 of the Bank for International Settlements (BIS, the so-called central bankers' bank), devoted to "promoting global monetary and financial stability" at a moment when "there is no respite for the global economy," buffeted by the COVID pandemic and then the war in Ukraine.[26] Though reminiscent of the 1970s, the current situation is novel in combining high inflation with record debt—corporate, personal, and governmental—and high asset prices. The fundamental problem, the bank's analysis suggests, is low growth internationally. Ultimately, restoring the economic growth the BIS sees as slowed by inflation will require "reigniting growth-friendly expenditure, in particular investment and supply-side reforms."[27] Meanwhile, however, it is crucial to understand the mechanics of inflation, to "look under the hood," as the BIS writers put it, to see how to regulate the economic engine.

Under the hood, they distinguish between low-level inflation in the form of relative price changes and what they call "inflation itself," which comes into existence as those relative changes affect each other and begin to move together. While "the recent broadening of inflation pressures suggests that many firms have greater pricing power than they did pre-pandemic," the transition from "low-level" to "sustained" inflation "ultimately involves a self-reinforcing feedback between price and wage increases." Price increases, they assert, "cannot be self-sustaining without feedback between prices and wages," because "profit margins and real wages cannot fall indefinitely," (46) though they do not explore how much higher than wages prices can go before life for wage-earners becomes intolerable. On the other hand, "once wage–price spirals set in, they develop an inertia that is not easy to break," except by using monetary policy to impose high levels of unemployment. "Thus, a key challenge for the central bank is to avoid transitions from low- to high-inflation regimes in the first place—to nip inflation in the bud." (61) In other words, in the absence of any near-term prospect of increased investment and enlarged supply, even in the absence of significant real wage growth there is "a premium on a prompt monetary policy response" (63) constricting demand by way of an induced recession, especially since "we may be reaching a tipping point." (xi) There is a danger, according to the BIS, that "As existing wage agreements expire, workers are likely to seek larger wage rises. In some countries they have already secured wage indexation clauses to guard against future inflation surprises." (14) If wages rise, prices simply must rise as well, if profitability is to be maintained, Like Jerome Powell, the BIS fears a possible future wage–price spiral.

It is true that the degradation of working-class living standards—the foundation, along with booming asset prices, of the extreme inequality of income and wealth achieved in recent decades—has begun to meet some response around the world, in the form of small-scale attempts at unionization, strike movements of increasing amplitude, and even a surprisingly large withdrawal of workers from the labor market in the face of poor working conditions at sub-subsistence pay. Is the Bank for International Settlements sensing a potential threat to the upper hand that employers now have over their employees, in a context of low or stagnant growth and increasing economic and therefore political conflict, not to mention a rapidly developing set of climate catastrophes? At any rate, their approach to inflation treats it as anything but a primarily monetary issue, nor as a matter to be dealt with by policy choices carefully adjusting theoretically determined natural rates of interest and unemployment to restore the supply–demand equilibrium supposedly basic to the market economy. It is the manifestation of a struggle between businesses mobilizing their pricing power to maintain profit levels and workers—at a structural and imaginative disadvantage, thanks to decades of neoliberalism—just beginning to react to the shifting onto their shoulders of capitalism's failures. Competitive inflation represents a struggle over into whose hands the social product will flow, but in the absence of a significant burst of investment it cannot increase the quantity of that product that counts as profit other than by lowering real wages.

Money and Violence

Meanwhile, the happy assumption of Magic Money—in Sebastian Mallaby's words, "the expectation that took hold in the late 1990s, that the Fed could be relied upon to cushion the economy from almost any type of shock"—has been replaced by general agreement that "the Fed [and other central banks] may have to run tighter policy than in the past quarter of a century."[28] Despite the disappearance of any theoretical consensus about the outer limits of national indebtedness and the expansion of bank (and nonbank) credit facilities, there remains a suspicion among economists and government officials that money can't just be handed out indefinitely without any problems. Despite the irrealism of economic theory, in particular with respect to the nature of money, this suspicion has a basis in the fact that the financial system to which the bulk of policymakers' efforts is directed is part of an economy that must continue to produce material goods and services and realize—turn into money—the profits that production makes possible. Though the stock and bond values vaporized in periodic crashes can be replenished by central banks, capitalist society cannot keep going without the steady production of goods and services that can be sold to yield returns reinvested in plant, equipment, and labor able to generate yet more value and profit. That is, the "real economy" and money are—to say it once again—indissoluble aspects of one system.

Financial instruments represent claims on future profits; for those claims to be realized, goods must be produced and sold. If capitalists can't make enough money to pay their workers enough to afford the rents or mortgages on their homes, for example, mortgage-based bonds and venture-capital investments in real estate will not turn a profit. Housing prices will eventually collapse, as they did in 2008, and the money invested in them will disappear.

Every period of prosperity involves the extension of credit to a point at which it outstrips the ability of profit production to support repayment—especially if, as Marx argued, profitability has a tendency to decline. This is why business-cycle downturns appear as banking and stock-market crashes as well as the sudden appearance of unsalable goods and unemployable workers. The postwar expansion of government deficit spending and private credit-money creation has overlaid a relatively permanent version of this process on the cyclical pattern, making capitalism itself into a sort of Ponzi scheme. It is this that appears both in the unstoppable postwar growth of debt and in the periodic monetary, banking, and securities crises that punctuate it.

To give a minor illustration of this point, the fortune of whoever is proclaimed at one moment or another "the world's richest person" today is for the most part financial, defined largely by stock prices. These prices move to a significant degree independently of the underlying value-productivity of the enterprises that issue them, reflecting investors' guesses about their future levels, in addition to a host of less rational factors (hence Marx, following a nineteenth-century English banker, called them "fictitious capital"). It is the combination of financial engineering—what economic historian Robert Brenner cleverly called "asset-bubble

Keynesianism"—and the tendential immiseration of the bulk of the world's population that has made possible the concentration of wealth, real and fictitious, in a diminishing percentage of hands, despite a low-growth economy. But if, say, Bernard Arnault of LVMH attempted to turn the improbable $211 billion with which he is credited into cash, the very attempt to sell the stock he owns in his company would send its value to a much lower level. The fortunes of such entrepreneurs, like the capitalization of the leading tech companies, the world's most valuable, are products of the Age of Credit—now grossly expanded into Magic Money—not the Age of Money, which was capitalism's period of ascension.

Yet, if Magic Money will someday really come to an end, it must be asked: when will the reckoning it has helped put off come due? The answer is that it has been coming due, and paid for, for decades. The recurrent bubble pops, in which thousands, millions, and even billions of dollars evaporate from the accounts of individuals and institutions are, we could say, down payments on the accumulating unpayable debt. The 2022 collapse of the FTX cryptocurrency exchange was a spectacular example; more significant was the capitalization collapse of the over-leveraged Adani Group, which lost $110 billion in five days in early 2023 (in the process reducing the personal fortune of Gautam Adani, at the time the "world's third richest man," by half, to $61 billion). But down payments are also to be seen in the steady worsening of the working and living conditions of the world's waged workers, though these are not reported in relation to particular financial events. Instead, they appear in such phenomena as the disappearance from Sri Lanka in 2022 of the funds necessary to buy fuel or food; the hollowing out of financial institutions in Lebanon; the mounting inability of the English working class to pay for heating in winter; incipient mass starvation in Somalia and Afghanistan; and rising poverty levels in the United States. The coming recession—or stagnation, if fear of social upheaval powers another surge of Magic Money—will simply be an acceleration of this tendency, even as some of the money generated in the last go-round is burned off. The new trillions poured out by the state will be intended as an accompaniment to austerity, not an alternative to it.

This state of affairs came into clear view when the u.s. authorities responded to the 2023 depositors' run on Silicon Valley Bank by guaranteeing all deposits. No doubt this was partially due to the pleas of those depositors—tech businesspeople central to the tech sector, a thousand of whom met virtually with Joshua Frost, the u.s. Treasury's assistant secretary for financial markets—that they embodied American economic dynamism. When shortly thereafter Swiss bank regulators forced a merger between the collapsing Credit Suisse and UBS, bondholders were given a $17 billion haircut (though equity owners kept some of their money) but the Swiss National Bank offered a liquidity backup line of SFr100 billion. In the case of SVB, the bank's troubles were due in part directly to the Fed's increasing of interest rates to fight inflation, an effort counteracted by preventing depositor losses.

In Ruchir Sharma's clear-eyed summary of the situation,

> More than low interest rates, the easy money era was shaped by an increasingly automatic state reflex . . . to rescue the economy from disappointing growth even during recoveries, to rescue not only banks and other companies but also households, industries, financial markets and foreign governments in times of crisis.

The latest bank runs show that the easy money era is not over. Inflation is back so central banks are tightening, but the rescue reflex is still gaining strength. The stronger it grows, the less dynamic capitalism becomes ... Government intervention eases the pain of crises but over time lowers productivity, economic growth and living standards.[29]

At the same time, the u.s Federal Reserve, along with other central banks, continued their anti-inflationary raising of interest rates. The will to put an end to the era of Magic Money coexists with an unwillingness to accept its consequences for the business economy.

The rapid rise of hunger, homelessness, forced migration, and mass health crises in the richest countries as well as the poorest is a reminder that violence has other modalities of appearance than the earlier standbys of clubs and bullets. But events in the economically weaker countries, such as Nigeria, Iran, Somalia, Chile, Egypt, Peru, and Sri Lanka, in which mass uprisings have been met with military force, show us that these methods have not been consigned to the past. Alexis Moraitis has traced the postwar arc from prosperity to austerity as it unfolded in France. In that country as in many others,

Threats of military putsches, a growing feeling of insecurity, and increased state violence are symptomatic of the entrenched economic decline that has gripped France. Like in most advanced countries, growth has been slowing down for several decades now. The French economy is not expanding as fast as it used to, thus failing to guarantee

economic security and welfare for all. As the production
of value is petering out, struggles over the distribution
of existing resources become more intense, threatening
social stability. Stagnation creates an environment con-
ducive to witch-hunting as France looks for the sources
of its downfall in migrant hordes, religious minorities,
or young rioters.[30]

An inflationary spiral, in which wage gains were recouped
by corporate price increases, was tolerable in the thirty years that
followed the Second World War, as France participated in the
general expansion of the world economy. After 1980, however,
"The inflationary compromise of the post-war era broke down,
as French elites made the choice of European monetary integration precisely in order to choke off the inflationary tendencies
of the domestic economy and check income growth." The result
is that the wish to guarantee social peace has run into declining
capacity to pay for it:

> In a context of intensifying stagnation, state elites find that
> existing tools for managing social discontent are quickly
> becoming obsolete and are forced to devise alternative
> ways of pursuing economic reform despite social resist-
> ance. As the carrot of social spending has become too
> expensive and the stick of European budget rules has
> proven too soft, the recourse to the crude repression of
> social resistance appears as a tantalizing option for des-
> perate reformers unable to gather popular consent for
> their painful policies.[31]

The correctness of the underlying analysis here was demonstrated in early 2023 by the nation-wide strikes and protests set off by the Macron government's decision to "reform" the pension system by changing the age limit for access to full pensions from 62 to 64, overwhelmingly opposed by popular opinion. The government met the protests with increasingly violent police action.

The United States was a pioneer of the use of policing and imprisonment as a substitute for the welfare state, as President Lyndon Johnson's "War on Poverty" gave way to incarceration in the 1970s as a solution to the problem of increasingly unemployable masses of people.[32] Fifty years later, the limits of this solution appeared in the nationwide riots (echoed internationally) provoked by the police killings of George Floyd and many others. Both the strategy and its limits appear almost everywhere in the world today, as state violence is met with rising social discontent and the varied socio-political responses, from neo-fascist stirrings to demands for the abolition of the police, in which it takes form.

Historian Steve Fraser devoted a book, *The Age of Acquiescence*, to the question of how the lively u.s. tradition of anti-capitalist class struggle gave way to an acceptance of the existing social system as the only realistic framework for achieving an enjoyable life.[33] In this he made an important, because historically grounded, contribution to such postwar attempts to understand the decline of radical consciousness as Herbert Marcuse's *One-Dimensional Man* (1964) and Guy Debord's *Society of the Spectacle* (1967). Fraser locates the turning point, convincingly, in the New Deal, when the federal government made a real effort, however inadequate it was, to respond to the privations visited by the depression on the American working class. Although his focus is on the United States, the story is, as we have seen, a global one: the Age of Acquiescence coincided with the Age of Credit, which was also the Age of Inflation—with the attempt to mobilize government deficit spending, monetary policy, and private money-creation to offset the capitalist dynamic that produces periodic social hardship for the wage-earning majority.

Basic to this period, whatever the changing modes of economic theorizing, was the recognition in practice of the integral place of money in the existing system of production and distribution that has evolved since the sixteenth century as a relation between waged workers and their capitalist employers subordinated to the production of money profits. Despite the neoclassical depiction of that system as constituted by a set of exchanges between property owners, it has always been clear to those on both sides of the capital–wage labor relation that the system's welfare depends on a relation between money profits and money wages making possible the continued growth of capital investment. Despite its closer approach to reality, the Keynesian attempt to construe that growth as one of "national income" regulable by an appropriate use of money by the state, as representative of the general interest, to balance investment and consumption also misrepresented the actual nature of capitalism. The goal of production in this mode of social organization is not actually "growth"— the enlarged creation of consumable goods—but enterprises' competitive accumulation of control over social resources in the form of money: the accumulation of capital. With the failure of the system to establish the equilibrium decreed by theory to be its normal state, governments have attempted to use monetary means—based on taxing, spending, and borrowing—to bring it about. But government spending, as we have seen, leads to the accumulation not of capital but of debt; the continuing decline of profitability results in a continuing low level of investment, in place of which the demand for profit requires greater pressure on the working and living conditions of the world's producing classes.

An integral part of the capitalist mechanism, money in itself neither is the source of nor provides a solution to capitalism's ills. Policymakers' obsession with its management by central banks or fiscal policy is a substitute for facing the actual dynamic of the social system. Let us remember: the main function of monetary exchange as a central social institution is to block access of the producers to their product except on pain of submitting for another day, week, month, to working for the enrichment of the owners of productive enterprises. For over a hundred years, this has seemed to most people the preferable alternative to the difficulties and mortal dangers inherent in challenging that state of affairs. After all, creating a new social order will require both taking social power away from those who have it now and constructing new methods for regulating economic life not based on the valuation of goods in money terms. Whether people will stick with acquiescence as the inherent limits of capitalist development shift the balance from credit-based social management to violence is an open question. The accelerating ecological effects of the unbridled quest for monetary gain—which governs owners of capital as well as their employees—may well be another factor prompting the abolition of a society that has made money its central mystery. Difficult though it still may be to imagine it, as this social order had a historical beginning, it can certainly be brought to an end.

REFERENCES

Introduction

1 Rachel Siegel, "Where's the Economy Headed? To Quote the Fed Chief, 'Hard to Say,'" *Washington Post*, November 5, 2022.

2 See Paul Mattick, *Social Knowledge: An Essay on the Nature and Limits of Social Science*, 2nd edn (London, 2021).

3 *The Telegraph*, November 5, 2008.

4 *The Guardian*, July 26, 2009.

5 Matt Phillips, "We Have Crossed the Line Debt Hawks Warned Us About for Decades," *New York Times*, August 21, 2020.

6 Jim Tankersley, "How Washington Learned to Embrace the Budget Deficit," *New York Times*, May 16, 2020.

7 J. H. Tankersley, "Federal Borrowing Amid Pandemic Puts U.S. Debt on Path to Exceed World War II," *New York Times*, September 2, 2020.

8 V. Golle, O. Rockeman, and R. Pickert, "Why Economists Got it Wrong on U.S. Inflation," *LA Times*, November 11, 2021.

9 J. Smialek, "Powell Says Fed is Ready to Raise Rates if Needed," *New York Times*, January 12, 2022, p. B3.

10 J. B. Rudd, "Why Do We Think that Inflation Expectations Matter for Inflation? (And Should We?)," Finance and Education Discussion Series 2021-062 (Washington, DC: Board of Governors of the Federal Reserve System, 2021); https://doi.org/10.17016/FEDS.2021.062.

11 R. J. Schiller, "Why Do People Dislike Inflation?" NBER Working Paper 5539 (Cambridge, 1996).

1 Money, Goods, and Prices

1 F. Braudel, *Civilization and Capitalism, 15th–18th Century*, vol. III: *The Perspective of the World*, trans. Sian Reynolds (New York, 1984), p. 75.

2 Ibid., p. 221.

3 Ibid., p. 386.

4 Ibid., p. 356.

5 K. Marx, *Capital*, vol. 1 (Harmondsworth, 1977), p. 223.

6 For a brief survey of classical Chinese paper money and inflation, see Peter Bernholz, *Monetary Regimes and Inflation: History, Economic and Political Relationships*, 2nd edn (Cheltenham, 2015), pp. 60–69.

7 G. Ingham, *The Nature of Money* (London, 2004), p. 127.

8 In this they were following the example of John Law, the Scottish gambler and cardsharp who in 1716 had convinced the Regent Philippe d'Orléans, himself a notable gambler, that he could satisfy the French crown's chronic need for cash. A royal edict authorized Law to establish a bank with a capital of 6 million livres. The bank made loans—largely to the government—in the form of notes, convertible into metal currency. The expansion of credit offered by the bank led to an economic boom. When the Regent proposed additional loans, Law raised money by selling stock in a company promising to extract gold deposits imagined to exist in Louisiana, along with other enterprises. Shares rose; the funds flowed through the royal government to individuals who bought more shares in Law's Mississippi Company. Since the gold did not exist, the scheme functioned only so long as new money flowed in. In 1720, large-scale investor conversions of notes into gold led to a run on the bank and its total collapse.

9 R. Skidelsky, *Money and Government: The Past and Future of Economics* (New Haven, CT, 2018), pp. 394–5.

10 J. K. Galbraith, *Money: Whence It Came, Where It Went* (Princeton, NJ, 2017), p. 69.

11 Bruce G. Carruthers and Sarah Babb, "The Color of Money and the Nature of Value: Greenbacks and Gold in Postbellum America," *American Journal of Sociology*, CI/6 (1996), p. 1575.

12 C. Bresciani-Turroni, *The Economics of Inflation: A Study of Currency Depreciation in Post-War Germany, 1914–1923*, trans. Millicent E. W. Savers (New York, 1937), p. 286.

13 *Gold and the Currency: Specie Better than Small Bills* (Boston, MA, 1855), cit. Michael F. Bryan, "On the Origin and Evolution of the Word *Inflation*," Federal Reserve Bank of Cleveland, October 15, 1997.

14 See the data assembled in David H. Fischer, *The Great Wave: Price Revolutions and the Rhythm of History* (Oxford, 1996), pp. 156ff.

15 Many authorities today do not count this as a depression; thus Skidelsky describes it as "not a depression in the modern sense, rather a lingering deflationary disease, punctuated by bursts of excitement" (*Money and Government*, p. 51). The compendium of contemporary descriptions of business difficulties, unemployment, and mass impoverishment in David A. Wells's fascinating *Recent Economic Changes and Their Effect on the Production and Distribution of Wealth and the Well-Being of Society* (New York, 1890) certainly suggests where the idea of a long depression came from.

16 Christopher Anstey, "Larry Summers Warns of a Dreaded Economic 'Doom Loop,'" *Fortune*, November 21, 2022 (https://fortune.com/2022/10/21/larry-summers-warns-doom-loop-deficit-interest-rates-economy).

2 The Age of Inflation

1 Numbers from Gianni Toniolo, "Europe's Golden Age, 1950–1973," *Economic History Review*, LI/2 (1998), p. 252. As just pointed out, the numbers should be taken with a large grain of salt.

2 C. Maier, "Inflation and Stagnation as Politics and History," in *The Politics of Inflation and Economic Stagnation*, ed. Leon N. Lindberg and C. Maier (Washington, DC, 1985), pp. 3–34.

3 Thus Angus Maddison asserts, in *The World Economy in the 20th Century* (Paris, 1989), that a "major cause of the worldwide inflation was the breakdown of the Bretton Woods arrangements which had provided a fixed exchange rate, dollar based, international monetary system" (p. 86).

4 In the United States, characteristically, it was even considered to demonstrate "a great nation's moral qualities, as a shining exemplification of its progress in civilization, as a marked indication of its possession of that first of Christian values, upright and downright honesty" (Elliot C. Cowdin, *Historical Sketch of Currency and Finance: An Address Delivered Before the Citizens of Cincinnati, Ohio in Robinson's Opera House, June 12, 1876* [Cincinnati, OH, 1976], p. 52).

5 Ben Bernanke and Harold James, "The Gold Standard, Deflation, and Financial Crisis in the Great Depression," in *Financial Markets and Financial Crisis*, ed. R. Glenn Hubbard (Chicago, IL, 1991), p. 41.

6 R. O. Keohane, "The International Politics of Inflation," in *The Politics of Inflation*, ed. Lindberg and Maier, p. 83.

7 See Herbert Stein, *The Fiscal Revolution in America* (Chicago, IL, 1969), p. 89

8 Adam Tooze, *The Wages of Destruction: The Making and Breaking of the Nazi Economy* (New York, 2006), p. 47.

9 Stein, *Fiscal Revolution*, p. 170.

10 Ibid., p. 172.

11 For a prescient discussion, see Paul Mattick, "The Keynesian International," *Contemporary Issues*, II/8 (1951), pp. 299–311.

12 Robert M. Collins, *The Business Response to Keynes, 1929–1964* (New York, 1981), pp. 81–2.

13 M. Salvati, "The Italian Inflation," in *The Politics of Inflation*, ed. Lindberg and Maier, p. 515.

14 Cit. Stein, *Fiscal Revolution*, p. 184.

15 U.S. Congress, Joint Committee on the economic report, *Federal Tax Policy for Economic Growth and Stability*, 84th Cong., 1st sess., 1955, p. 233, cit. Stein, *Fiscal Revolution*, p. 363.

16 Rudolf Klein, "Public Expenditure in an Inflationary World," in *The Politics of Inflation*, ed. Lindberg and Maier, p. 205.

17 Franklin D. Roosevelt, *The Public Papers and Addresses of Franklin D. Roosevelt*, vol. III (New York, 1938), p. 47, cit. Stein, *Fiscal Revolution*, p. 42. This is more or less what today's dollars, Federal Reserve notes, are.

18 Stein, *Fiscal Revolution*, pp. 180, 394.

19 Ibid., p. 344.

20 Maddison, *The World Economy in the 20th Century*, p. 85.

21 F. Braudel, *Civilization and Capitalism, 15th–18th Century*, vol. III: *The Perspective of the World*, trans. Sian Reynolds (New York, 1984), p. 618.

22 For the numbers see P. Mattick, *Business as Usual: The Economic Crisis and the Failure of Capitalism* (London, 2011), p. 57.

23 "Transcript of Reagan Address Reporting on the State of the Nation's Economy," *New York Times*, February 6, 1981, cit. David R. Cameron, "Does Government Cause Inflation? Taxes, Spending, and Deficits," in *The Politics of Inflation*, ed. Lindberg and Maier, p. 224.

24 G. W. Domhoff, *The Myth of Liberal Ascendancy* (London, 2013), p. 157.

25 W. Carl Biven, *Jimmy Carter's Economy: Policy in an Age of Limits* (Chapel Hill, NC, 2002), p. 242, cit. Domhoff, *Myth of Liberal Ascendancy*, p. 230.

26 Robert Brenner, "What is Good for Goldman Sachs Is Good for America: The Origins of the Present Crisis" (UCLA: Center for Social Theory and Comparative History, 2009; https://escholarship.org/uc/item/0sg0782h), p. 6.

27 Mattick, *Business as Usual*, p. 74.

3 Theories and Policies

1 Cit. David H. Fischer, *The Great Wave: Price Revolutions and the Rhythm of History* (Oxford, 1996), p. 84.

2 Hume, "Of Money," *Essays and Treatises on Several Subjects* (Edinburgh, 1758), vol. I, p. 164.

3 D. Ricardo, *Reply to Mr Bosanquet's Observations on the Report of the Bullion Committee* (London, 1811), p. 91.

4 Ibid., pp. 93, 94.

5 G. von Haberler, *Prosperity and Depression* (Geneva, 1937), p. 167.

6 For a careful account of the neoclassical debt to mathematical physics, see Philip Mirowski, *More Heat Than Light: Economics as Social Physics, Physics as Nature's Economics* (Cambridge, 1989). Thomas M. Humphrey finds "the most important contributing factor" to the dominance of the Quantity Theory in turn-of-the-century economics in "the rigorous mathematical restatement of the quantity theory provided by neo-classical economists . . . [which] added substantially to the intellectual appeal and scientific prestige of the theory" ("The Quantity Theory of Money: Its Historical Evolution and Role in Policy Debates," Federal Reserve Bank of Richmond *Economic Review* (May–June 1974), pp. 12–13).

7 J. A. Schumpeter, *History of Economic Analysis* (London, 1954), p. 1088.

8 I. Fisher, "Our Unstable Dollar and the So-Called Business Cycle," *Journal of the American Statistical Association*, XX (1925), pp. 191, 201, cit. W. C. Mitchell, *Business Cycles: The Problem and Its Setting* (New York, 1927), p. 129.

9 Ben Bernanke and Harold James, "The Gold Standard, Deflation, and Financial Crisis in the Great Depression," in *Financial Markets and Financial Crisis*, ed. R. Glenn Hubbard (Chicago, IL, 1991), p. 41.

10 C. Romer, "What Ended the Great Depression?," *Journal of Economic History*, LII/4 (1992), p. 757.

11 Henryk Grossmann, "Marx, Classical Economics, and the Problem of Dynamics," trans. P. Mattick, *International Journal of Political Economy*, XXXVI/2 (2007), p. 43.

12 K. Wicksell, *Vorlesungen über Nationalökonomie auf Grundlage des Marginalprinzips* (Jena, 1920), vol. II, pp. 241–2; R. G. Hawtrey, *Wärung und Kredit* (Jena, 1926), p. 124; both cit. Grossmann, "Marx, Classical Economics, and the Problem of Dynamics," p. 43.

13 J. M. Keynes, *The General Theory of Employment Interest and Money* (New York, 1936), p. 9.

14 For an incisive treatment of the relation between the development of governmental economic action and Keynesian theory in the U.S. during the New Deal period, see Herbert Stein, *The Fiscal Revolution in America* (Chicago, IL, 1969), ch. 7.

15 Keynes, *General Theory*, p. 27.

16 Ibid., p. 293.

17 "If there is an increased investment in any given type of capital during any period of time, the marginal efficiency of that type of capital will diminish as the investment in it is increased, partly because the prospective yield will fall as the supply of that type of capital is increased, and partly because, as a rule, pressure on the facilities for producing that type of capital will cause its supply price to increase; the second of these factors being usually the more important in producing equilibrium in the short run, but the longer the period in view the more does the first factor take its place." This is because "the only reason why an asset offers a prospect of yielding during its life services having an aggregate value greater than its initial supply price is because it is *scarce* . . ." (Keynes, *General Theory*, pp. 136, 213).

18 Keynes, *General Theory*, p. 30.

19 Ibid., p. 104.

20 M. Campbell, "Marx and Keynes on Money," *International Journal of Political Economy*, XXVII/3 (1997), p. 79.

21 Keynes, *General Theory*, pp. 321, 219.

22 Ibid., pp. 381, 374.

23 Ibid., p. 309.

24 Paul Mattick, *Marx and Keynes* (Boston, MA, 1969), p. 21. This work remains the fundamental Marxian critique of Keynesian theory, and informs much of the present book, along with the same author's *Economics, Politics and the Age of Inflation* (London, 1978).

25 R. Skidelsky, *Money and Government: The Past and Future of Economics* (New Haven, CT, 2018), p. 130.

26 Stein, *Fiscal Revolution*, p. 163.

27 Ibid., p. 167.

28 While mathematicized neoclassical economics made its breakthrough into academic respectability in the decade of the Depression, it achieved dominance in professional journals in the postwar period; see P. Mirowski, "The When, the How and the Why of Mathematical Expression in the History of Economic Analysis," *Journal of Economic Perspectives*, v/1 (1991), p, 151 and *passim*.

29 Stein, *Fiscal Revolution*, pp. 464–5.

30 See A. W. Phillips, "The Relationship Between Unemployment and the Rate of Change of Money Wages in the United Kingdom, 1861–1957," *Economica*, 25 (1958), pp. 283–99.

31 Skidelsky, *Money and Government*, p. 137.

32 As Thomas Mayer explains, echoing Hume's conception of the immediate versus long-term effects of inflation in a comment on the Monetarist interpretation of the Phillips Curve, "if there exists only a very short-run trade-off between unemployment and inflation such intervention would do little good." T. Mayer, ed., *The Structure of Monetarism* (New York, 1978), p. 36.

33 M. Friedman, "Japan and Inflation," *Newsweek*, September 4, 1978, p. 75.

34 Harry G. Johnson, "Comment on Mayer on Monetarism," in *The Structure of Monetarism*, ed. Mayer, p. 131.

35 M. Friedman and Anna Jacobsen Schwartz, *A Monetary History of the United States, 1867–1960* (Princeton, NJ, 1963), p. 300.

36 Johnson, "Comment on Mayer on Monetarism," p. 131. In Friedman's words: "the past record of stability in the United States . . . offers much support for the view that, if the monetary framework were stable, our private enterprise economy is sufficiently adaptable to the other changes that occur to yield a high degree of economic stability in the short run as well as the long run . . . [What is needed] is to keep monetary changes from being a destabilizing force . . . by assigning the monetary authorities the task of keeping the stock of money growing at a regular and steady rate, month in and month out." "Monetary Theory and Policy," statement before the Joint Economic Committee,

86th Congress, 1st Session, May 25–8, 1959, in *Inflation: Selected Readings*, ed. R. J. Ball and P. Doyle (Harmondsworth, 1969), pp. 144–5.

37 M. Friedman, "The Demand for Money: Some Theoretical and Empirical Results," *Journal of Economic Policy*, LXVII/4 (1959), p. 351.

38 M. Friedman, "The Role of Monetary Policy," *American Economic Review*, LVIII/1 (1968), p. 12.

39 G. Ingham, *The Nature of Money* (London, 2004), p. 30.

40 William Greider, *Secrets of the Temple: How the Federal Reserve Runs the Country* (New York, 1989) pp. 454–5.

41 In the colorful words of British economist Nicholas Kaldor, "The great revival of 'monetarism' in the 1970s, culminating in the adoption of the strict prescriptions of the monetarist creed by a number of Western governments at the turn of the decade ... will, I am sure, go down as one of the most curious episodes in history, comparable only to the periodic outbreaks of mass hysteria (such as the witch hunts) of the Middle Ages." "How Monetarism Failed," *Challenge*, XXVIII/2 (1985), p. 4.

42 A representative, and measured, summary by one contemporary specialist: "the inflationary consequences of increasing the money supply are historically indeterminate, though usually the price rise was ... less than proportional to the increase in the monetary stock, except when severe debasements created a veritable 'flight from coinage,' when coined money was exchanged for durable goods." John Munro, review of *American Treasure and the Price Revolution in Spain, 1501–1650*, https://eh.net, 2007.

43 David A. Wells's fascinating *Recent Economic Changes and Their Effect on the Production and Distribution of Wealth and the Well-Being of Society* (New York, 1890), p. 205.

44 See W. C. Mitchell, "The Quantity Theory of the Value of Money," *Journal of Political Economy*, IV/2 (1896), pp. 139–65. Examining the theory both theoretically and empirically, Mitchell concluded that "from either point of view, the theory seems to be defective" (p. 165). Mitchell returned to the topic in the context

of his doctoral dissertation on greenbacks and then in the course of his lifelong study of business cycles; for a look at his work in the context of the controversy over the Quantity Theory at the turn of the century see Abraham Hirsch, "Wesley Clair Mitchell, J. Lawrence Laughlin, and the Quantity Theory of Money," *Journal of Political Economy*, LXXV/6 (1967), pp. 822–43.

45 Karl Marx and Frederick Engels, *Collected Works*, vol. XXIX: *A Contribution to the Critique of Political Economy* (London, 1987), p. 395.

46 Ibid., p. 400.

47 Ibid., pp. 404–5. For a brilliant discussion of the role played by Marx's disproof of the Quantity Theory in the construction of his own theory of money, see M. Campbell, "Marx's Explanation of Money's Functions: Overturning the Quantity Theory," in *Marx's Theory of Money: Modern Appraisals*, ed. F. Moseley (London, 2005), pp. 143–59.

48 Marx, *A Contribution to the Critique of Political Economy*, p. 415.

49 K. Marx, *Capital*, vol. I (Harmondsworth, 1976), p. 220. Ricardo's follower James Mill, for instance, states the Quantity Theory in precisely these terms. Modern quantity theorists evade this criticism by invoking a mechanism, usually some version of an excessive demand for goods attendant on an increase in the money supply, linking the latter to inflation.

50 Ibid., p. 237. See W. C. Mitchell, *Business Cycles: The Problem and Its Setting* (Washington, DC, 1927), pp. 130ff.

51 O. Morgenstern, *On the Accuracy of Economic Observations*, 2nd edn (Princeton, NJ, 1963), p. 96.

52 See the discussion in Mitchell, *Business Cycles*, pp. 128ff.

53 Friedman, "The Role of Monetary Policy," p. 8.

54 W. David Slawson, *The New Inflation: The Collapse of Free Markets* (Princeton, NJ, 1981), p. 163.

55 Friedman and Schwartz, *Monetary History*, p. 300.

56 David R. Cameron, "Does Government Cause Inflation?," in *The Politics of Inflation*, ed. Lindberg and Maier, p. 278.

57 M. Friedman, "Quantity Theory of Money," in *The New Palgrave: A Dictionary of Economics*, ed. John Eatwell et al.

(London, 1987), vol. IV. S. Weintraub had a more brutal response: "If unemployment is the answer to the inflation problem, then Keynesianism as a social philosophy is dead, literally interred by Keynesians and, curiously, all in the name of the mentor." "The Keynesian Theory of Inflation: The Two Faces of Janus?," *International Economic Review*, 1 (1960), pp. 143–55; reprinted in *Inflation*, ed. Ball and Doyle, p. 72.

58 Ingham, *The Nature of Money*, p. 31.

59 Loretta J. Mester, "The Role of Inflation Expectations in Monetary Policymaking: A Practitioner's Perspective," European Central Bank Forum on Central Banking: Challenges for Central Bank Policy in a Rapidly Changing World (Sintra, Portugal, June 29, 2022).

60 According to the founding father of this doctrine, Georg F. Knapp, "The state as guardian of the law declares that the property of being the means of payment should be inherent in certain stamped pieces [of paper as well as metal] as such, and not in the material of the pieces." *The State Theory of Money*, trans. H. M. Lucas and J. Bonar (London, 1924), p. 39. Schumpeter's brief comment is sufficient and definitive: "[Knapp's] theory was simply a theory of the 'nature' of money considered as the legally valid means of payment. Taken in this sense it was as true and as false as it is to say, for example, that the institution of marriage is a creation of law." *History of Economic Analysis*, p. 1090.

61 Stephanie Kelton, *The Deficit Myth: Modern Monetary Theory and the Birth of the People's Economy* (New York, 2021), pp. 43, 47.

4 Modern Money

1 See the useful survey by Maurice Flamant and Jeanne Singer-Kérel, *Modern Economic Crises and Recessions* (New York, 1970).

2 In Mitchell's words, though earlier forms of social life are not "free from crises, or from alternations of good and bad times . . . until a large part of the population is living by getting and

spending money incomes, producing wares on a considerable scale for wide markets, using credit devices, organizing in business enterprises with relatively few employers and many employees, the economic fluctuations which occur do not have the characteristics of business cycles." W. C. Mitchell, *Business Cycles: The Problem and Its Setting* (New York, 1927), p. 75; see pp. 75–82.

3 Mitchell, *Business Cycles*, pp. 62, 63, 86.

4 Ibid., p. 64.

5 This assumption is visible across economic theory, for instance in the use of "capital" to mean both tools used in production processes and the money used in capitalism to buy them, or in Thomas Piketty's calculation of the profitability of capital from ancient Rome to the present. A periodically fashionable version of the assumption is Karl Polanyi's idea that "the economy" is "embedded" in earlier modes of social life, emerging only in capitalism as a visibly distinct social subsystem.

6 Present-day barter transactions among businesses—there were around 450,000 such transactions in the United States in 2010, according to the International Reciprocal Trade Association— are managed by calculating the money values of the goods exchanged; the bartering of cryptocurrencies on the Etherium platform is based on similar calculations.

7 This is why neoclassical economics, which attempts to explain money prices as functions of subjective valuations of commodities, is forced to assume the "law of one price" to render "utilities" comparable; see Philip Mirowski, *More Heat Than Light: Economics as Social Physics, Physics as Nature's Economics* (Cambridge, 1989), pp. 236–8.

8 As he puts it in a footnote in the first volume of *Capital*, "it does not occur to the economists that a purely quantitative distinction between the kinds of labour"—as is implied by the equation of the materializations of these kinds to quantities of money—"presupposes their qualitative unity or equality, and therefore their reduction to abstract human labour": K. Marx, *Capital*, vol. 1 (Harmondsworth, 1976), p. 173 n. 33.

An analogous problem arises for the neoclassical attempt to derive money-denominated values from individual "utilities" or preferences: in Ingham's words, how can "an *inter*-subjective scale of value (money of account) emerge from myriad subjective preferences?" G. Ingham, *The Nature of Money* (London, 2004), p. 25.

9 See "Labour," in Raymond Williams, *Keywords: A Vocabulary of Culture and Society*, revd edn (New York, 1985), pp. 177–9.

10 Ingham, *The Nature of Money*, p. 6.

11 K. Marx, "Original Text," in K. Marx and F. Engels, *Collected Works*, vol. XXIX (London, 1987), p. 431.

12 See F. Braudel, *The Structures of Everyday Life* (New York, 1981), ch. 7; *The Wheels of Commerce* (New York, 1982), ch. 1.

13 Karl Marx reported on these events for the *New York Tribune* in 1857, mocking the Bank Act as "a self-acting principle for the circulation of paper money according to which the latter would exactly conform its movement of expansion and contraction to the laws of a purely metallic circulation, and all monetary crises . . . would thus be warded off for all time to come." "The Bank Act of 1844 and the Monetary Crisis in England," in K. Marx and F. Engels, *Collected Works*, vol. XV (London, 1986), p. 379. Reviewing this material as part of his study of the credit system in the manuscript of the third volume of *Capital*, Marx stressed the practical disproof of the Quantity Theory and the Ricardian conception of money bound up with it; see K. Marx, *Capital*, vol. III (Harmondsworth, 1993), pp. 680ff.

14 When the British government resumed gold convertibility in 1925, "British prices were too high, causing competitive difficulties for the textile exporters of Lancashire and for import-competing chemical firms. Sterling's overvaluation depressed the demand for British goods, aggravating unemployment. It drained gold from the Bank of England, forcing it to raise interest rates even at the cost of depressing the economy." B. Eichengreen, *Globalizing Capital: A History of the International Monetary System* (Princeton, NJ, 1996), p. 59.

15 See the discussion ibid., Ch. 4.

16 The crisis occasioned by the COVID-19 pandemic in 2020, however, produced circumstances so abnormal that the U.S. Federal Reserve System was forced to buy large quantities of Treasuries to support the price and enable international liquidity.

17 This may be vaguely measured by share of world GDP; in 2020 the USA's share was well over 20 percent; China was second with 15 percent; Germany had less than 4 percent and Russia less than 2 percent. This hierarchy is even more prominent with regard to the market value of companies listed in national equity markets: in 2013 the USA came in at over $24,000 billion, China at $7,000 billion, and Japan at $4,500 billion. See table 7.2 in Tony Norfield, *The City: London and the Global Power of Finance* (London, 2016), p. 181 and chap. 5 *passim*.

18 As concisely expressed by Mattick in *Marx and Keynes* (Boston, MA, 1969), "Behind monetary transactions stand the capital values of business firms . . . as material entities in their commodity form," p. 173.

19 As we shall see in the next chapter, the supply of money is further enlarged by the production of "shadow money," credit instruments basic to the contemporary financial system.

20 Marx, *Capital*, vol. I, p. 181.

21 The eminent late nineteenth-century economist Karl Menger famously explained the origin of money in just this fashion: see "On the Origin of Money," *Economic Journal*, II/6 (1892), pp. 239–55.

22 Marx, *Capital*, vol. III, p. 707.

23 D. Foley, "Marx's Theory of Money in Historical Perspective," in *Marx's Theory of Money: Modern Appraisals*, ed. Fred Moseley (London, 2005), p. 48.

24 For a closer discussion of the representation of productive activity by money, see ch. 5 of P. Mattick, *Theory as Critique: Essays on 'Capital'* (Chicago, IL, 2019).

25 O. Morgenstern, *On the Accuracy of Economic Observations*, 2nd edn (Princeton, NJ, 1963), pp. 183, 193.

26 Bureau of Labor Act, U.S. Statutes at Large 23 (1885), p. 60, cit. Darren Rippy, "The First Hundred Years of the Consumer Price

Index: A Methodological and Political History," U.S. Bureau of
Labor Statistics *Monthly Labor Review*, April 2014, https://doi.
org/10.21916/mlr.2014.13.

27 Ibid., p. 27.

28 Ibid., p. 66.

29 Ibid., p. 119.

30 Morgenstern, *On the Accuracy of Economic Observations*, p. 190.

31 J. A. Schumpeter, *History of Economic Analysis* (London, 1954),
p. 759.

32 Federal Reserve Bank of Minneapolis, "Consumer Price Index,
1800–," www.minneapolisfed.org.

33 Helen MacFarlane and Paul Mortimer-Lee, "Inflation over 300
Years," Bank of England *Quarterly Bulletin* (1994 Q2), p. 157.

5 Prices and Profits

1 R. Paxton, *The Anatomy of Fascism* (New York, 2004), p. 137.

2 B. Eichengreen, *Globalizing Capital: A History of the
International Monetary System* (Princeton, NJ, 1996), p. 95. In
fact, according to Eichengreen, the late nineteenth-century
success of the gold standard rested on the insulation of national
states from domestic politics, with falling wages facilitated by
the absence of "universal male suffrage and the rise of trade
unionism and parliamentary labor parties" which later "polit-
icized monetary and fiscal policymaking" (p. 4). A related
development, which came with the development of fractional-
reserve banking, was the need for central banks to intervene
as "lenders of last resort" in moments of financial crisis, also
incompatible with the foreign-exchange stability central to the
gold-standard regime (see pp. 36–7).

3 W. C. Mitchell, *Business Cycles: The Problem and Its Setting*
(New York, 1927), pp. 106, 107.

4 The common-sense conclusion is statistically supported by Jose
A. Tapia, "Profits Encourage Investment, Investment Dampens
Profits, Government Spending Does Not Prime the Pump:
A DAG Investigation of Business-Cycle Dynamics," May

2015; https://mpra.ub.uni-muenchen.de/64698/1/MPRA_
paper_64698.pdf.

5 Daniel M. Hausman, *Capital, Profits, and Prices: An Essay
in the Philosophy of Economics* (New York, 1981), p. 191.

6 Hence Schumpeter, accepting general-equilibrium theory
as an abstract description of the capitalist economy (*Über die
mathematische Methode der theoretischen Ökonomie. Zeitschrift
für Volkswirtschaft, Sozialpolitik und Verwaltung* [Vienna, 1906])
invented a separate theory to account for the system's cyclical
dynamics, framed in terms of the disruptive personality of entrepreneurs who recurrently initiate disequilibrating processes of
"creative destruction." (*Theorie der wirtschaftlichen Entwicklung*
(Berlin, 1911)).

7 For a brief history of business-cycle theory see ch. 2 of
P. Mattick, *Business as Usual: The Economic Crisis and the Failure
of Capitalism* (London, 2011).

8 Mitchell, *Business Cycles*, p. 173. It should be said that Mitchell's
lack of allegiance to theory was based on a deep knowledge
of the subject, as is attested by the lectures collected in
W. C. Mitchell, *Types of Economic Theory, From Mercantilism
to Institutionalism*, ed. Joseph Dorfman, 2 vols (New York,
1969).

9 This is an extreme simplification of a complicated argument. For
a discussion of some of the complications, see P. Mattick, *Theory
as Critique: Essays on 'Capital'* (Chicago, IL, 2019), ch. 10.

10 For an astute discussion of these issues, see Jason E. Smith,
*Smart Machines and Service Work: Automation in a Age of
Stagnation* (London, 2020), Ch. 5 and *passim*.

11 For a detailed version of this argument see Paul Mattick, *Marx
and Keynes* (Boston, MA, 1969).

12 As a percentage of GDP U.S. national debt went from 33 percent
in 1976 to 120 percent in 2022. See Federal Reserve Bank of
St Louis, "Federal Debt: Total Public Debt as Percent of Gross
Domestic Product," https://fred.stlouisfed.org.

13 See Rudolf Klein, "Public Expenditure in an Inflationary
World," in *The Politics of Inflation and Economic Stagnation*,

ed. Leon N. Lindberg and C. Maier (Washington, DC, 1985), pp. 196–223.

14 For a book-length version of this argument see A. Tooze, *Crashed: How a Decade of Financial Crises Changed the World* (New York, 2018).

15 FOMC *Minutes*, June 8, 1971, p. 50, cit. Christina D. Romer and David H. Romer, "The Evolution of Economic Understanding and Postwar Stabilization Policy," NBER Working Paper 9274 (October 2002), p. 26. The absence of the Great Depression from Burns's two-sentence history is striking.

16 Don. R. Conlan, "Gauging the True Growth of Profitability," *New York Times*, August 4, 1974.

17 W. David Slawson, *The New Inflation: The Collapse of Free Markets* (Princeton, NJ, 1981), pp. 96–7.

18 "U.S. Farm Income Outlook: December 2020 Forecast," Congressional Research Service, February 9, 2021, https://crsreports.congress.gov, p. 2.

19 Slawson, *The New Inflation*, p. 104. The Canadian trade union official and writer Charles Levinson put it in these terms in 1971: "When turnover falls off, instead of prices being cut to bolster sales and restore income, as the textbooks propound, the loss in income is compensated through upward price adjustments at the lower volume. This is feasible because of the general price inelasticity of most consumer products and the administered price systems pervasive throughout industry. In the U.S., the least cartelized and presumably the most open-market economy in the world, 80 percent of consumer prices are administered by agreements—overt or covert. In Europe the myth of price competition is not taken seriously by anyone." *Capital, Inflation, and the Multinationals* (New York, 1971), p. 214.

20 Slawson, *The New Inflation*, pp. 146–7. An interesting version of this strategy appeared in China in the 1990s, when the programmatic shift from centrally set to market-determined prices ran into a problem of pervasive deflation. In response, "Heeding calls from increasingly powerful large firms, both state-owned and private, and pushed by its own interests, the government

condoned and encouraged the formation and enforcement of price cartels organized by firms, associations, and industrial ministries." A conscious imitation of practices in the USA, Europe, and especially Japan, this attempt was only partially successful, largely because of comparatively low levels of industrial concentration. Scott Kennedy, "The Price of Competition: Pricing Policies and the Struggle to Define China's Economic System," *China Journal*, 49 (2003), p. 2.

21 D. K. Foley, "On Marx's Theory of Money," *Social Concept*, 1/12 (1983), p. 18.

22 M. Schularick and A. Taylor, "Credit Booms Gone Bust: Monetary Policy, Leverage Cycles, and Financial Crises, 1870–2008," *American Economic Review*, CII/2 (2012), p. 1058. We have already noted this effect in the failure of the Monetarist attempt to control the supply of funds available to business by regulating the Fed's money creation.

23 M. Aglietta and A. Orléan, *La violence de la monnaie* (Paris, 1984), p. 252.

24 For an analytically sophisticated survey, see Daniela Gabor and Jacob Vestergaard, "Towards a Theory of Shadow Money," Institute for New Economic Thinking working paper, April 2016, www.ineteconomics.org. "Repo"—repurchase agreements—refers to short-term (for example, overnight) exchanges of securities, such as government bonds, for cash, with a promise to repurchase at a specified date. In the USA by 2022, $2 to $4 trillion was traded in the repo market daily. The collapse of Lehman Brothers in 2008, a turning point in the unfolding of the financial crisis, was triggered by the bank's loss of access to repo financing.

25 Schularick and Taylor, "Credit Booms Gone Bust," p. 1031; "leverage" means debt employed in investment to expand the sum of money actually in hand.

26 Ibid., p. 1038.

27 For an interesting account of inflationary cycles in China as the product of competition for power between political factions within the Chinese Communist Party, see Victor C. Shih,

Factions and Finance in China: Elite Conflict and Inflation (Cambridge, 2008); here party-determined investment produces growth-stimulated price increases analogous to those produced by boom periods in earlier European and American capitalism.

28 Ruchir Sharma, "This Is How the Coronavirus Will Destroy the Economy," *New York Times*, March 16, 2020, www.nytimes.com.

29 Joseph Baines and Sandy Brian Hager, "COVID-19 and the Coming Corporate Debt Catastrophe," SBHager.com, March 13, 2020, https://sbhager.com.

30 OECD, "Corporate Bond Debt Continues to Pile Up," February 18, 2020, www.oecd.org. Debt levels have only increased since then.

31 I borrow the term "extra money" in this context from Michael De Vroey's exceptionally clear and suggestive article, "Inflation: A Non-Monetarist Monetary Interpretation," *Cambridge Journal of Economics*, VIII/4 (1984), pp. 381–99.

6 From the Great Inflation to Magic Money

1 David R. Cameron, "Does Government Cause Inflation? Taxes, Spending, and Deficits," in *The Politics of Inflation and Economic Stagnation*, ed. Leon N. Lindberg and C. Maier (Washington, DC, 1985), p. 264.

2 Ibid., p. 266.

3 Ibid., pp. 267–9.

4 William Greider, *Secrets of the Temple: How the Federal Reserve Runs the Country* (New York, 1989), p. 710.

5 K. Rogoff, "Impact of Globalization on Monetary Policy," in *The New Economic Geography: Effects and Policy Implications* (Kansas City, MO, 2007), p. 269.

6 Ibid., p. 274.

7 Akio Mikuni and R. Taggart Murphy, *Japan's Policy Trap: Dollars, Deflation, and the Crisis of Japanese Finance* (Washington, DC, 2002), p. 33.

8 "Central government debt, total (% of GDP) for Japan," available at https://fred.stlouisfed.org, accessed February 23, 2023.

9 This was printing money not, as in 1920s Germany, to pay government debts but to expand them.

10 A. Lowrey, "The Great Affordability Crisis Breaking America," *The Atlantic*, February 2020. The concept and estimate of financial fragility comes from a study at George Washington University funded by the National Endowment for Financial Education; see "Financial Fragility in the U.S.: Evidence and Implications," 2018, www.nefe.org.

11 Juan M. Sanchez and Hee Sung Kim, "Why Is Inflation So Low?," Federal Reserve Bank of St. Louis *Regional Economist*, February 2, 2018, www.stlouisfed.org.

12 Thomas Hasenzagi, Filippo Pellegrino, Lucrezia Reichlin, and Giovanni Ricco, "The Inflation Puzzle in the Euro Area—It's the Trend Not the Cycle!" VOX.CEPR Policy Portal, October 16, 2019, https://voxeu.org.

13 Phillip Inman, "Japan's Economy Heading for Recession, and Germany Wobbles," *The Guardian*, February 17, 2020, www.theguardian.com; "U.S. Economic Growth Flat in Final Three Months of 2019," *CBS News* update, January 30, 2020, www.cbsnews.com. These data should, as usual, be taken with a grain of salt, but they serve to indicate trends.

14 S. Gandel, "What to Expect as Corporate Giants Report Earnings for Fourth Quarter," *New York Times*, January 14, 2022, p. B5.

15 M. Aglietta and A. Orléan, *La violence de la monnaie* (Paris, 1984).

16 Ibid., pp. 190–91, 220. Emphasizing the inability of the Quantity Theory to explain this event, these authors observe that "this experience flagrantly contradicts the traditional schemas for exiting inflationary situations: diminution of the monetary mass, decrease in demand, improvement of the balance of trade. Exactly the opposite occurred . . ." (p. 218).

17 Rachel Siegel, "Two Blocks from the Federal Reserve, a Growing Encampment of the Homeless Grips the Economy's Most Powerful Person," *Washington Post*, April 17, 2021.

18 "'I knew Paul Volcker,' Mr. Powell said during congressional testimony this month. 'I think he was one of the great public

servants of the era—the greatest economic public servant of the era.'" *New York Times*, March 14, 2022.

19 Ben Casselman, "Making Sense of an Economy Running Hot," *New York Times*, June 3, 2022.

20 Justin Jacobs, "ExxonMobil Swells Buybacks to $50bn Despite Rebuke over War-Fuelled Profits," *Financial Times*, December 9, 2022.

21 Isabella Simonetti and Julie Cresswell, "Rocketing Prices of Food Elevate Company Profits," *New York Times*, November 2, 2022, p. 1.

22 It was invented by Franco Modigliani and Lucas Papademos in 1975 as the NIRU (non-inflationary rate of unemployment); see F. Modigliani and L. Papademos, "Targets for Monetary Policy in the Coming Year," *Brookings Papers on Economic Activity*, 1 (Washington, DC, 1975), pp. 141–65.

23 In fact, Modigliani and Papademos insist, "In an exploration for direct correlations between money growth and inflation, the simplest relations fail. Year by year, the acceleration (or deceleration) of inflation and the acceleration (or deceleration) of money growth show no positive relation. In the post-Korean period these two variables moved more often in opposite directions than together, and the correlation between them for the 1953–71 period is about zero. Allowing for a one-year lag of prices behind money scarcely changes this result, with the correlation still only 0.08 and observations for nine out of twenty-one years going in the 'wrong' direction" (ibid., p. 160).

24 J. Powell, "Challenges for Monetary Policy," speech at a symposium sponsored by the Federal Reserve Bank of Kansas City, Jackson Hole, Wyoming, August 23, 2019.

25 Cit. Stephanie Kelton, *The Deficit Myth: Modern Monetary Theory and the Birth of the People's Economy* (New York, 2021), pp. 52–3.

26 Bank for International Settlements, *Annual Economic Report*, June 2022, www.bis.org, p. 28; subsequent page references are in parentheses in the text.

27 As the tautological character of this idea suggests, it would be truer to say that low growth is a cause of inflation.

28 Sebastian Mallaby, "The End of Magic Money: Inflation and the Future of Economic Stimulus," *Foreign Affairs*, July 11, 2022, www.foreignaffairs.com.

29 R. Sharma, "The Unstoppable Rise of Government Bailouts," *Financial Times*, March 27, 2023.

30 A. Moraitis, "Waking Up from Anesthesia: Decline and Violence in France," *Brooklyn Rail*, April 2022, https://brooklynrail.org.

31 Ibid.

32 See the discussion in Jarrod Shanahan and Zhandarka Kurti, *States of Incarceration: Rebellion, Reform, and America's Punishment System* (London, 2022), pp. 88ff.

33 S. Fraser, *The Age of Acquiescence: The Life and Death of American Resistance to Organized Wealth and Power* (New York, 2016).

SELECT BIBLIOGRAPHY

Aglietta, Michel, and A. Orléan, *La violence de la monnaie* (Paris, 1984)

Baines, Joseph, and Sandy Brian Hager, "COVID-19 and the Coming Corporate Debt Catastrophe," http://sBHager.com, March 13, 2020

Bank for International Settlements, *Annual Economic Report*, June 2022, www.bis.org

Bernanke, Ben, and Harold James, "The Gold Standard, Deflation, and Financial Crisis in the Great Depression," in *Financial Markets and Financial Crisis*, ed. R. Glenn Hubbard (Chicago, IL, 1991)

Bernholz, Peter, *Monetary Regimes and Inflation: History, Economic and Political Relationships*, 2nd edn (Cheltenham, 2015)

Braudel, Fernand, *The Structures of Everyday Life* (New York, 1981)

—, *The Wheels of Commerce* (New York, 1982)

—, *The Perspective of the World* (New York, 1984)

Brenner, Robert, "What Is Good for Goldman Sachs Is Good for America: The Origins of the Present Crisis," UCLA: Center for Social Theory and Comparative History, 2009, www.escholarship.org

Bresciani-Turroni, Costantino, *The Economics of Inflation: A Study of Currency Depreciation in Post-War Germany, 1914–1923*, trans. Millicent E. W. Savers (New York, 1937)

Bryan, Michael F., "On the Origin and Evolution of the Word *Inflation*," Federal Reserve Bank of Cleveland, October 15, 1997

Cameron, David R., "Does Government Cause Inflation? Taxes, Spending, and Deficits," in *The Politics of Inflation*, ed. Lindberg and Maier

Campbell, Martha, "Marx and Keynes on Money," *International Journal of Political Economy*, XXVII/3 (1997)

—, "Marx's Explanation of Money's Functions: Overturning the Quantity Theory," in *Marx's Theory of Money: Modern Appraisals*, ed. F. Moseley (London, 2005)

Carruthers, Bruce G., and Sarah Babb, "The Color of Money and the Nature of Value: Greenbacks and Gold in Postbellum America," *American Journal of Sociology*, CI/6 (1996), pp. 1556–91

Collins, Robert M., *The Business Response to Keynes, 1929–1964* (New York, 1981)

Cowdin, Elliot C., *Historical Sketch of Currency and Finance: An Address Delivered Before the Citizens of Cincinnati, Ohio in Robinson's Opera House*, June 12, 1876 (Cincinnati, OH, 1976)

De Vroey, Michael, "Inflation: A Non-Monetarist Monetary Interpretation," *Cambridge Journal of Economics*, VIII/4 (1984), pp. 381–99

Domhoff, G. W., *The Myth of Liberal Ascendancy* (London, 2013)

Eichengreen, Barry, *Globalizing Capital: A History of the International Monetary System* (Princeton, NJ, 1996)

Federal Reserve Bank of Minneapolis, "Consumer Price Index, 1800–," www.minneapolisfed.org

Fischer, David H., *The Great Wave: Price Revolutions and the Rhythm of History* (Oxford, 1996)

Flamant, Maurice, and Jeanne Singer-Kérel, *Modern Economic Crises and Recessions* (New York, 1970)

Foley, Duncan K., "On Marx's Theory of Money," *Social Concept*, I/12 (1983)

—, "Marx's Theory of Money in Historical Perspective," in *Marx's Theory of Money: Modern Appraisals*, ed. Fred Moseley (London, 2005)

Fraser, Steve, *The Age of Acquiescence: The Life and Death of American Resistance to Organized Wealth and Power* (New York, 2016)

Friedman, Milton, "The Demand for Money: Some Theoretical and Empirical Results," *Journal of Economic Policy*, LXVII/4 (1959), pp. 327–51

—, "The Role of Monetary Policy," *American Economic Review*, LVIII/1 (1968), pp. 1–17

—, "Monetary Theory and Policy," statement before the Joint Economic Committee, 86th Congress, 1st Session, May 25–8, 1959, in *Inflation: Selected Readings*, ed. R. J. Ball and P. Doyle (Harmondsworth, 1969)

—, "Japan and Inflation," *Newsweek*, September 4, 1978

—, "Quantity Theory of Money," in *The New Palgrave: A Dictionary of Economics*, ed. John Eatwell et al. (London, 1987)

Friedman, Milton, and Anna Jacobsen Schwartz, *A Monetary History of the United States, 1867–1960* (Princeton, NJ, 1963)

Gabor, Daniela, and Jacob Vestergaard, "Towards a Theory of Shadow Money," Institute for New Economic Thinking working paper, April 2016, www.ineteconomics.org

Galbraith, John Kenneth, *Money: Whence It Came, Where It Went* (Princeton, NJ, 2017)

Greider, William, *Secrets of the Temple: How the Federal Reserve Runs the Country* (New York, 1989)

Grossmann, Henryk, "Marx, Classical Economics, and the Problem of Dynamics," trans. P. Mattick, *International Journal of Political Economy*, XXXVI/2 (2007), pp. 6–83

Haberler, Gottfried von, *Prosperity and Depression* (Geneva, 1937)

Hasenzagi, Thomas, Filippo Pellegrino, Lucrezia Reichlin, and Giovanni Ricco, "The Inflation Puzzle in the Euro Area—It's the Trend Not the Cycle!" VOX.CEPR Policy Portal, October 16, 2019, www.cepr.org

Hausman, Daniel M., *Capital, Profits, and Prices: An Essay in the Philosophy of Economics* (New York, 1981)

Hirsch, Abraham, "Wesley Clair Mitchell, J. Lawrence Laughlin, and the Quantity Theory of Money," *Journal of Political Economy*, LXXV/6 (1967)

Hume, David, "Of Money," *Essays and Treatises on Several Subjects*, vol. 1 (Edinburgh, 1758)

Humphrey, Thomas M., "The Quantity Theory of Money: Its Historical Evolution and Role in Policy Debates," Federal Reserve Bank of Richmond *Economic Review*, May–June 1974

Ingham, Geoffrey, *The Nature of Money* (London, 2004)

Johnson, Harry G., "Comment on Mayer on Monetarism," in *The Structure of Monetarism*, ed. Mayer

Kaldor, Nicholas, "How Monetarism Failed," *Challenge*, XXVIII/2 (1985)

Kelton, Stephanie, *The Deficit Myth: Modern Monetary Theory and the Birth of the People's Economy* (New York, 2021)

Kennedy, Scott, "The Price of Competition: Pricing Policies and the Struggle to Define China's Economic System," *China Journal*, 49 (2003)

Keohane, R. O., "The International Politics of Inflation," in *The Politics of Inflation*, ed. Lindberg and Maier

Keynes, John Maynard, *The General Theory of Employment Interest and Money* (New York, 1936)

Klein, Rudolf, "Public Expenditure in an Inflationary World," in *The Politics of Inflation*, ed. Lindberg and Maier

Knapp, Georg F., *The State Theory of Money*, trans. H. M. Lucas and J. Bonar (London, 1924)

Levinson, Charles, *Capital, Inflation, and the Multinationals* (New York, 1971)

Lindberg, Leon N., and C. Maier, eds, *The Politics of Inflation and Economic Stagnation* (Washington, DC, 1985)

Lowrey, Annie, "The Great Affordability Crisis Breaking America," *The Atlantic*, February 2020

MacFarlane, Helen, and Paul Mortimer-Lee, "Inflation over 300 Years," Bank of England *Quarterly Bulletin* (1994 Q2)

Maddison, Angus, *The World Economy in the 20th Century* (Paris, 1989)

Maier, Charles, "Inflation and Stagnation as Politics and History," in *The Politics of Inflation*, ed. Lindberg and Maier

Mallaby, Sebastian, "The End of Magic Money: Inflation and the Future of Economic Stimulus," *Foreign Affairs*, July 11, 2022, www.foreignaffairs.com

Marx, Karl, *Capital*, vol. I (Harmondsworth, 1976)

—, "[The Bank Act of 1844 and the Monetary Crisis in England],"
in K. Marx and F. Engels, *Collected Works*, vol. XV (London, 1986)

—, *A Contribution to the Critique of Political Economy*, in Karl Marx
and Frederick Engels, *Collected Works*, vol. XXIX (London, 1987)

—, "Original Text," in K. Marx and F. Engels, *Collected Works*,
vol. XXIX (London, 1987)

—, *Capital*, vol. III (Harmondsworth, 1993)

Mattick, Paul, *Marx and Keynes* (Boston, MA, 1969)

—, *Economics, Politics and the Age of Inflation* (London, 1978)

—, *Business as Usual: The Economic Crisis and the Failure of
Capitalism* (London, 2011)

—, *Theory as Critique: Essays on* Capital (Chicago, IL, 2019)

—, *Social Knowledge: An Essay on the Nature and Limits of Social
Science*, 2nd edn (London, 2021)

Mayer, Thomas, ed., *The Structure of Monetarism* (New York, 1978)

Menger, Karl, "On the Origin of Money," *Economic Journal*, II/6
(1892)

Mester, Loretta J., "The Role of Inflation Expectations in Monetary
Policymaking: A Practitioner's Perspective," European Central
Bank Forum on Central Banking: Challenges for Central Bank
Policy in a Rapidly Changing World (Sintra, Portugal, June 29,
2022)

Mikuni, Akio and R. Taggart Murphy, *Japan's Policy Trap: Dollars,
Deflation, and the Crisis of Japanese Finance* (Washington, DC,
2002)

Mirowski, Philip, *More Heat Than Light: Economics as Social Physics,
Physics as Nature's Economics* (Cambridge, 1989)

—, "The When, the How and the Why of Mathematical Expression
in the History of Economic Analysis," *Journal of Economic
Perspectives*, V/1 (1991), pp. 145–57

Mitchell, Wesley Clair, "The Quantity Theory of the Value of
Money," *Journal of Political Economy*, IV/2 (1896), pp. 139–65

—, *Business Cycles: The Problem and Its Setting* (New York, 1927)

—, *Types of Economic Theory, From Mercantilism to Institutionalism*,
2 vols, ed. Joseph Dorfman (New York, 1969)

Modigliani, Franco, and L. Papademos, "Targets for Monetary Policy in the Coming Year," *Brookings Papers on Economic Activity*, 1 (Washington, DC, 1975)

Moraitis, Alexis, "Waking Up from Anesthesia: Decline and Violence in France," *Brooklyn Rail*, April 2022, https://brooklynrail.org

Morgenstern, Oskar, *On the Accuracy of Economic Observations*, 2nd edn (Princeton, NJ, 1963)

Munro, John, review of *American Treasure and the Price Revolution in Spain, 1501–1650*, https://eh.net, 2007

Norfield, Tony, *The City: London and the Global Power of Finance* (London, 2016)

OECD, "Corporate Bond Debt Continues to Pile Up," February 18, 2020, www.oecd.org

Paxton, Robert O., *The Anatomy of Fascism* (New York, 2004)

Phillips, A. W., "The Relation Between Unemployment and the Rate of Change of Money Wage Rates in the United Kingdom, 1861–1957," *Economica*, 25 (1958), pp. 283–99

Ricardo, David, *Reply to Mr Bosanquet's Observations on the Report of the Bullion Committee* (London, 1811)

Rippy, Darren, "The First Hundred Years of the Consumer Price Index: A Methodological and Political History," U.S. Bureau of Labor Statistics *Monthly Labor Review*, April 2014, doi.org/10.21916/mlr.2014.13

Romer, Christina, "What Ended the Great Depression?," *Journal of Economic History*, LII/4 (1992), pp. 757–84

—, and David H. Romer, "The Evolution of Economic Understanding and Postwar Stabilization Policy," NBER Working Paper 9274 (October 2002)

Roosevelt, Franklin D. *The Public Papers and Addresses of Franklin D. Roosevelt*, vol. III (New York, 1938)

Rudd, J. B., "Why Do We Think that Inflation Expectations Matter for Inflation? (And Should We?)," Finance and Education Discussion Series 2021-062 (Washington: Board of Governors of the Federal Reserve System, 2021); doi.org/10.17016/FEDS.2021.062

Salvati, Michele, "The Italian Inflation," in *The Politics of Inflation*, ed. Lindberg and Maier

Sanchez, Juan M., and Hee Sung Kim, "Why Is Inflation So Low?," Federal Reserve Bank of St. Louis *Regional Economist*, February 2, 2018, www.stlouisfed.org

Schiller, Robert J., "Why Do People Dislike Inflation?" NBER Working Paper 5539 (Cambridge, 1996)

Schularick, M., and A. Taylor, "Credit Booms Gone Bust: Monetary Policy, Leverage Cycles, and Financial Crises, 1870–2008," *American Economic Review*, CII/2 (2012), pp. 1029–61

Schumpeter, Joseph A., *History of Economic Analysis* (London, 1954)

Shanahan, Jarrod, and Zhandarka Kurti, *States of Incarceration: Rebellion, Reform, and America's Punishment System* (London, 2022)

Sharma, Ruchir, "The Unstoppable Rise of Government Bailouts," *Financial Times*, March 27, 2023.

Shih, Victor C., *Factions and Finance in China: Elite Conflict and Inflation* (Cambridge, 2008)

Skidelsky, Robert, *Money and Government: The Past and Future of Economics* (New Haven, CT, 2018)

Slawson, W. David, *The New Inflation: The Collapse of Free Markets* (Princeton, NJ, 1981)

Smith, Jason E., *Smart Machines and Service Work: Automation in an Age of Stagnation* (London, 2020)

Stein, Herbert, *The Fiscal Revolution in America* (Chicago, IL, 1969)

Tapia, Jose A., "Profits Encourage Investment, Investment Dampens Profits, Government Spending Does Not Prime the Pump: A DAG Investigation of Business-Cycle Dynamics," May 2015; https://mpra.ub.uni-muenchen.de/64698/1/MPRA_paper_64698.pdf

Toniolo, Gianni, "Europe's Golden Age, 1950–1973," *Economic History Review*, LI/2 (1998), pp. 252–67

Tooze, Adam, *The Wages of Destruction: The Making and Breaking of the Nazi Economy* (New York, 2006)

—, *Crashed: How a Decade of Financial Crises Changed the World* (New York, 2018)

Weintraub, Sidney, "The Keynesian Theory of Inflation: The Two Faces of Janus?," *International Economic Review*, 1 (1960), reprinted in *Inflation: Selected Readings*, ed. R. J. Ball and P. Doyle (Harmondsworth, 1969)

Wells, David A., *Recent Economic Changes and Their Effect on the Production and Distribution of Wealth and the Well-Being of Society* (New York, 1890)

Williams, Raymond, *Keywords: A Vocabulary of Culture and Society*, revd edn (New York, 1985)

ACKNOWLEDGMENTS

Martha Campbell, Duncan Foley, Jamie Merchant, Jason E. Smith, and Jose Tapia kindly read early drafts of this book and made helpful suggestions. Pavlos Roufos started me off with an invaluable list of suggested readings. Katy Siegel, as always, was a usefully critical discussant, from first to last.

INDEX